The

INDENTURED SERVANTS

from Bengal to Bush Lot to Belize

by

Karan Chand
B.A., DIP. Ed., M.Ed., OCT

DEDICATION

Dedicated to all bonded servants and victims of human trafficking who were, and those who still are, exploited everywhere and who made it possible

and

my family:
immediate and extended.

PREFACE

This historical-fiction is intended to educate, inform and sporadically entertain readers about some of the experiences of Indian indentured servants and their descendants. It preserves, for posterity, in this age of wireless, automated technology, snapshots of the struggles of some of our foreparents. Based on research, oral history and personal experiences, it covers three generations (one century) of struggles and resilience in a desperate effort to stay afloat and, for some, to soar.

Most of the available books on indentureship are serious, academic texts intended for the studious. Consequently, the general public, outside of academia, are only peripherally aware of the plight during this 'new form of slavery'. This novel is an attempt to capture and present the vicissitudes of life of some of our ancestors, in a user-friendly format, and reach out to more readers. The intermittent, fictional comic relief is in no way intended to trivialize the ordeal of a struggling people since the generic, overall experience is factual and was extremely dehumanizing.

While some of the characters and episodes are fictional, others actually existed; thus the label: historical-fiction. In some instances real names have been used and no defamation is intended to any person, living or deceased.

Karan Chand

CONTENTS

"If you know your history, then you'll know where you're coming from."

Bob Marley
Buffalo Soldier

1

Caught in Calcutta

The year was 1893. It was noon in Calcutta. The humid tropical climate was unbearably hot with temperatures over one hundred degrees Fahrenheit. Even so, the narrow streets were jam-packed with people going about their daily activities. Most of them were walking, while many were pushing handcarts or riding larger carts pulled by pairs of yoked oxen. The wealthy ones were under the canopies of rickshaws pulled by sinewy, barefooted, half-naked men who, despite the appearance of being frail, jogged on tirelessly. Amid them, cyclists were

richshaw

skillfully negotiating their way, carrying huge bundles of belongings balanced precariously on their handlebars and heads. As they proceeded, they carefully avoided squatting cows which sat nonchalantly, pensively chewing their cud with their heads raised in a seemingly defiant demeanor, as if aware of their sacred position of prominence.

Pedestrians, the street smarts, moved silently and briskly, helping to create the hustle and bustle of urban life. Sharks in their own right, they knew how to live, not merely exist, off the streets. They passed others, some naïve, chattering with their companions, careless in their deportment yet mindful of not stepping on dirt or dung. Some were vending sweetmeats and trinkets from their overburdened carts or from sidewalk stands beckoning people to patronize them in high-pitched, penetrating voices.

Near an intersection, a group of untidy beggars, hands outstretched, followed a coach drawn by two thoroughbred horses as it moved off. Increasing speed, the more energetic and optimistic outdistanced the pack as in a race of *Lime and Spoon* as the coach accelerated until it left them in disappointment behind. Just moments before, a wealthy traveler onboard had given one beggar a few rupees causing others to spontaneously gather for similar generosity.

On the sidewalk, under the awnings, other people were resting, lying on the ground. Some were eating snacks bought from the hawkers, who peddled all around, or merely swatting ubiquitous flies that were continually circling and landing. Adolescents and younger children were everywhere, in and out of the crowds, unsupervised. In their youthful innocence most of them were unaffected by the stress, responsibilities, uncertainties and worries of older people.

Even though he was in his mid-teens, however, Mattai was not in the mainstream. Circumstances had made his state of being and mind different from other happy-go-lucky children. Unlike most of them he was very tired, thirsty, and troubled. Moreover, he was unsure of his exact location, having lost his way in the busy, congested maze of streets while looking for hours for odd jobs. Exhausted, he sat on a stack of sacks tentatively watching the mass of people passing by, too timid to ask for directions. Everyone seemed occupied, intent on something.

His family was new in Calcutta, having moved there just two weeks before. Mattai desperately needed to find work. His father, who was not old but prematurely aged, was ill with TB and usually dizzy with high blood pressure. At fourteen, Mattai was the eldest child, his siblings being eleven and nine. His father did odd jobs occasionally but it was not enough to support the improvised family. Mattai felt obligated to do something for his family as other boys, some younger than him, were doing. In the countryside, where they had lived not long before, life had been tough. It did not rain for months at a time and consequently their crops did not grow well on the rocky, arid soil. When it did rain, it poured drowning their crops and assaulting their vulnerable, porous, flimsy shack, especially in the monsoon season. Their only recourse was to barricade themselves with jute bags which they slept on, then sleep on flattened cardboard boxes placed on the cold earthen floor. Often, the rainstorm continued for weeks flooding the entire village in knee-deep, muddy waters, forcing them to leave their house and seek refuge uphill. There, they would remain under the shelter of trees for several days, half-starved from eating only scarce fruits, dehydrated and shivering in the bitterly chilled winds.

As if that was not bad enough, they were always indebted to the unscrupulous local shop-keeper, Bugu, who overcharged them and constantly threatened to stop their credit, saying insultingly that he was not running an alms house.

"Whayuh think yuh doing, *gacchu*?"[1]
His brief respite was interrupted by a rough, unfriendly voice. He turned to face a dark, pudgy, cruel-looking man with glaring eyes.
" Ah… I am…."
"Yuh waan teef mi rice, yu *chore*!"[2] The man rolled his eyes as he spoke.
"No, ah jus..."
"Just! Ah kno' your kind, *chore*!" The man bellowed, grabbed him by his shredded shirt collar and pulled, causing it to rip, shedding two buttons.

---

[1] *Gacchu*-idiot/fool
[2] chore-thief

Passersby heard him and the more inquisitive ones stopped and surrounded them quickly, wanting to see what would happen next.

"This *haramé* [3] trie fuh teef mi rice," he continued even though no one had asked anything.

"Ah was just..."

"*Chore!*" someone from the crowd shouted. Mattai's heart raced and he became tongue-tied. He felt overwhelmed and defenseless, becoming speechless, unable to offer an explanation.

"Whas de matta?"

Heads turned and the crowd parted as a tall, athletic man in khaki uniform and beret came through.

"This *haramé* trie to teef mi rice," the fat man, his jaws shaking, said. Without any further question, the uniformed man said,

"Come with me," as he gestured with his baton.

Relieved, Mattai kept close to him as they walked away, glad to be rescued and removed by someone in authority.

"*Chore! chore!*" some in the crowd chorused as they left.

They stepped between packed, poverty-stricken people, clothed in rags, lying on the sidewalk. After about four minutes they turned into a side street and into an old cement structure which Mattai thought was a police station.

Upon entering the officer said, "I will jail you for stealing."

"But sahib, ah was just lookin fuh wuk." Mattai pleaded timidly.

---

[3] haramé-rogue/vagabond

"Wuk, wha kind of jaab yuh want?"

"Ahm...am...ah dono...any wuk, sahib." he stammered.

The man paced the room, baton under arm, then asked, "Stealing is wuk fu you?"

"No, sahib."

He went to a desk and riffled through a big book, then took a feather and wrote something, seeming to have forgotten Mattai's presence. Finally, he turned to Mattai and said,

"Today is you lucky day. You look like a good boy. Ah going to give yuh ah chance..."

"Thank you, sahib, I..."

"...and get you a jaab, sign this paypa."

"But, sahib, ah caan write."

Mattai's thumbprint was affixed to the paper and he was lead through the streets to a huge building which contained about two hundred people, adults

Holding Depot

and children. The police left him there with instructions not to leave. Mattai looked around. There was a long queue and people were giving out food at the head of it. He joined the line instinctively since he was starving. He was given some *alue* [4] curry and boiled rice piled on a torn, broad, thin leaf. Balancing it in one hand, he devoured it to the last grain. He then drank some water from a barrel nearby. Not familiar with anyone, he strolled over and sat by himself in a far corner. The meal had a soporific effect on him and in a short while he became drowsy and fell fast asleep.

---

[4] alue-Irish potato

2

Crossing 'Black Waters'

The angry, agitated crowd increased their chanting of "*Chore! Chore! Chore!*" and closed in on him. One dark, mean-looking, shirtless man with aquiline nose, piercing eyes and a huge mustache forced himself past the police and attempted to grab Mattai. Terrified and trembling, Mattiai stepped backward uncertainly then darted automatically under the railing behind him and ran through a narrow alleyway nearby, heart pounding. Several male members of the crowd rushed after him shouting, "*Chore! Chore!*" with the dark, mean-looking, big-mustached man in front. Mattai tried desperately to outpace them, driven by extreme desperation and a sudden surge of panic. As he glanced back furtively, he saw the man, outrunning the others, gaining on him. Unexpectedly, he stumbled and fell as the man, eyes glistening, reached out his claw-like hands...

He awakened traumatized, trembling, scared and covered in cold sweat. It was dark all around and he could not see anything. He felt the hard floor beneath him and wondered where he was. He came to realize that he was not at home in his bed which was equally hard but not wooden. He could hear hushed voices around but did not recognize any of them or what they were saying. He laid there in the darkness for what seemed like hours, not knowing what to do or say. He wanted to relieve himself but was afraid, hesitant and unsure where to go. At the same time, he was intimidated by his terrifying dream. He remained motionless, closing his eyes with the hopes of sleeping some more. He could not. Instead, he started to recall the day's events: leaving home...getting lost...being accused of stealing...afterwards, the police offering him a job and putting his fingerprint on a paper... then taking him to the building where he was given food. After that? He could not remember anything.

He wondered where he was. It was windy, dark and chilly. His thoughts drifted to his family. They must be out looking for him, getting anxious. In his entire life, he had never once stayed away from home overnight. They must be worried about him particularly since they had heard about the many horrifying crimes that occurred daily in Calcutta, especially at nights. He had to get back home as soon as possible. He had promised his mother to bring home a coconut and some oil which she need-ed to prepare the evening meal. Was she angry with him for not returning on time? He had always been obedient and cooperative, even proactive in doing chores which no one told him to do. The last thing he wanted was to disappoint his parents, least of all his mother. Tears came to his eyes as his thoughts raced through his mind. After a while he fell asleep once more.

Someone was shaking him, grabbing his shoulder. "Time to get up, get up!" a rough, uncom-passionate voice said as a firm grip rolled him to and fro. He opened his eyes slowly but the person had already moved on. He could not determine whether it was night or day. He wondered where he was. People, accompanied by music, were singing somewhere not far away. Becoming fully awake, he realized that he was lying on the floor of a large, almost dark building with older people nearby, chil-dren huddled against them. He rolled over and sat up. There were more people further away in all di-rections. As he focused, he identified an old bearded man, wearing a *pagri*, [5] not far away. He remem-bered seeing him in the large building where the police had taken him.

A ray of light was shining from a round window further away. He stood up and made his way towards it curiously. Outside, as far as he could see there was rough water. Large foam-crested

---

[5] pagri-turban

waves, bigger than any he had ever seen before, were moving away rapidly from below. He turned and proceeded to the other side, treading between still-sleeping people, and looked out of another window. There was never-ending water there also. In the distance, on the horizon, he saw a very small sailboat in silhouette but could not determine whether it was coming or going. He did no know what to make of it. After a while, he came to realize that they were in a big boat. He could not figure out anything else. Where were they and where were they going?

He looked at the people. They were all on the floor– no tables, benches or hammocks – lying, sitting or squatting. Some were in groups talking and occasionally laughing. There were mostly men. The few women had large sacks and cloth bundles they used as props and pillows. Further away in a corner one particular group was sitting in a circle singing and playing a *harmonium* [6], *dhantal* [7] and *dolack* [8], entertaining the crowd that surrounded them, many of whom clapped to the rhythm while a few were dancing. As the music continued non-stop, even those conversing, seemingly uninterested, stopped periodically to listen to a favorite song before continuing. Some even got up to dance

---

[6] harmonium-instrument with keyboard infront and the bellows of an accordian behind.

[7] dhantal-percussion instrument comprised of two short steel rods.

[8] dolak-two sided hand-drum slung over the neck.

whenever a 'danceable' song was sung, then sat back again. They seemed happy and contended as if enjoying an excursion. Only a few solitary ones, like Mattai, remained desolately by themselves.

After a short while he edged his way uncertainly towards a youth of his own age. He stood a short distance away, indecisively. Then he coughed evidently announcing his presence and, at the same time, clearing his throat as a prelude to speaking.

"Where wi goin ?" he finally asked.

"Wha yuh mean, where wi goin? To Afrikka."

"But ah noh waan tu go tu Afrikka," said Mattai

"Den jump in de wata and swim back."

Mattai did not have a response, not expecting such a retort.

"Yuh sign up tu go tuh Africa, right?" the youth continued.

"No," replied Mattai, "Ah whant tu stay in Calcutta, near home."

"Well, maybe yu noh read de paypa. Dis ship goin tu Africa."

Mattai immediately became depressed and lost all desire for further conversation. How did he get himself into this? Africa? Where is Africa? It cannot be far from home. How would his parents know where he was? This must be a mistake, a misunderstanding. He had not told the police that he wanted to go anywhere. It was surreal. He had to get someone to turn back the boat.

"Mi name Naidu." He was brought back to reality by the voice of the young man.

"Mi family going to Afrikka. Ova deh is mi ma, pa and sista." He gestured with his head in the direc-

12

tion of three people. Mattai looked at them speech-lessly. His sister, sitting on a box, was compellingly pretty. Under other circumstances he would have stolen glances at her frequently. Now he just hung his head, worried and uninterested.

"Wuk there fuh all of us; good pay too," Naidu re-sumed.

Mattai remained silent.

"Yu can get rich in five years."

"Well, ah waan tu go back home," Mattai repeated.

"Leh wi guh fuh some food," Naidu said, changing the topic and Mattai followed him submissively to join the line.

Unbeknownst to the deceived passengers the ship, *Hesperus*, was traveling in a southwesterly direction down the Bay of Bengal. Almost all of them were ignorant of their destination or the length of the journey they were undertaking. Some of them were under the impression that they going to the

Onboard ship during transcontinental voyage

"Company's Rabustie" not far away to do garden-ing. The agents who had kidnapped and induced them to go looked down on them condescendingly as animals hardly having any ideas beyond satisfying their basic needs, their base instincts, people without dignity, people to be deceived, people to be demeaned, the damned.

The ship weighed anchor at a seaport in Madras where more people came onboard while Mattai was sleeping during the night. Then it continued in the same direction for a while, passing between the Indian subcontinent and Ceylon,[9] before proceeding westwards.

During the days that followed, it traversed the Indian Ocean, turned in a south-westerly direction and bisected the waters between Madagascar and mainland Africa. The passengers crowded the upper deck as it docked at Durban on the east coast of South Bechuanaland.

Many people, including Naidu and his family disembarked. Mattai was not allowed to go ashore. He was roughly prevented by crewmen who

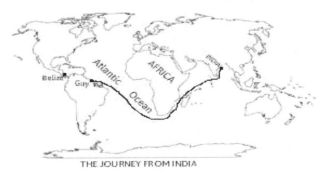

THE JOURNEY FROM INDIA

stood at the gangplank and permitted selected people from a list to leave. He watched helplessly as

---

[9] Ceylon-now called Sri Lanka

even a motionless person, covered on a stretcher, fetched by two crewmen and accompanied by a weeping woman, was taken ashore. His depression increased as he stood watching the long line of people leaving the ship. The only people he had got to know well in those ten days were departing. He wanted to make a break for it, to go with them, but knew that he would be slowed down by the congested crowd and be caught.

After four hours the ship weighed anchor and headed south then, after a while, west and eventually northwest as it passed the Cape of Good Hope. It had rounded the southern tip of Africa and was on its way to the West Indies as it proceeded to cross the Atlantic Ocean. The first stage of the journey, with its variable winds and cold southern winter lasted twenty six days.

In what seemed to be eternity to Mattai but was actually nine weeks the ship traversed the turbulent ocean, its huge cloth sales perpetually pregnant with the southeast trade winds. During that time he became acquainted with more people, bonding as unfamiliarity evolved into acceptance and then friendship. Though he was young and shy, or because of it, he was a good listener and learned what was really happening.

Some people on board had agreed to go to the West Indies which they thought was not far away over the waters. There, they would work for five years and then return with their earnings. The British who ruled India had many large farms there. There was plenty of easy work, high pay and housing for them in the West Indies —British Guiana, Jamaica, Trinidad, British Honduras and other strange sounding places. Thereafter, they will live in comfort for the rest of their lives. Why not make a short sacrifice for their families, they reasoned. This knowledge, especially the though of becoming rich, consoled Mattai somewhat but he was still overwhelmed by thoughts of being back with his family.

Some of the people onboard were with their families. Overtime, he became privy to more personal information. Among the crowd, there were some that were getting away from their spouse and abandoning their families. Mattai could not understand why people deserted their families considering that he had become homesick so quickly. A small number were fugitives, while some were eluding creditors who they could not repay. The majority was unemployed, poverty-stricken people coming from the barren hills of the West Bengal region of northeastern India. They had descended from the Rainagar and Durgapur areas to look for opportunities and a better life in Kolkata. That did not materialize. Among the diverse group, nonetheless there was one common factor: they all had great expectations.

As the days passed, Mattai mingled and mixed with more people, eating both the food they had brought, which some shared generously, and the one served on board. He sometimes played a game of cards. During the day people occupied the wind-swept, sunny upper deck.

However, at nights they went below where it was dark. Single women were placed in the rear of the ship with children and married couples in the middle. Unmarried men were accommodated in the forward area. All slept in the decks below where layers of lumber resembling huge, crude book-shelves topped by thin paillasses served as bunk beds. Everyone moved around cautiously trying not to invade the space of others in gloomy, congested quarters poorly lit with oil lamps. Only the rats enjoyed freedom of movement, which they blatantly flaunted, as if to emphasize the disparity, by continuously trespassing, sometimes running over them as they slept; at other times nibbling at their exposed toes.

After several weeks, the food that people brought with them ran out. At the same time, as if by some master plan, the meals given to them by the crew, invariably rice with *dhal* [10], became progressively scanty, tasteless and stale and people began to feel unwell. Many rapidly became infected with diarrhea, others fever, cholera or dysentery, while almost all became infested with ubiquitous lice. The few younger children feared worst. Together with the other illnesses, they became infected with rashes which they constantly scratched. No one seemed to be untouched by pestilence, spared of the epidemic on board. Additionally, lack of fresh water and the inability to bathe and change their clothes made everyone uncomfortable and itchy. Increas-

---

[10] dhal- boiled, seasoned yellow split peas.

ingly the floor, toilet area and sleeping quarters turned foul, filthy, unsightly and repelling. All the affected people were given one of two medications— two small, yellow pills or a brown, greasy balm— panacea for the poor, regardless of their symptoms. All the same, for the most part they were effective, probably because of the peoples' belief in them as a due to the placebo effect.

Over time people became less sociable, more irritable and progressively kept to themselves, hermit-like. Correspondingly, everyone became increasingly impatient to reach his or her destination, wanting an immediate end to the journey, this voyage of the damned.

Mattai could not find anyone who shared his feelings of wanting to go back home. Apparently everyone else was bent on ending this journey, or so he thought, as no one indicated that they had a change of heart. This was so because he was unaware that there was a group of rebellious captives locked beneath a section of the deck. With hatches bolted, they were constantly guarded over by 'Chokedars', vicious Indian men hired specifically for that purpose. Also, in order to have some semblance of order and to control them, they had earlier been divided into groups of about twenty five, each supervised by a *sardar* or headman appointed from among them. Moreover, there was a complement of cooks drawn from among the highest castes, and of sweepers drawn from the lowest. The crew members were called 'lascars', an Anglo-Indian word meaning sailors.

Integrated on board was four dozen or so Muslims who mixed and mingled with their fellow shipmates (*jihajis*) and only attracted casual attention as they stood, bowed, sat and prostrated themselves while praying several times each day.

One day Mattai was sitting by himself when a man approached him.

"Can yu spare mi some tobaca?" the man asked in a high-pitched voice. As Mattai turned to face him, he noticed that the man had two missing upper front teeth and a long, straight scar on his left jaw, extending from below his eye to his lip.

"Ah noh smoke," replied Mattai.

"Wha' yu think yu are, a *sadhu*?" [11] the man asked mockingly with a look of contempt.

Mattai became visibly angry when the man redeemed himself by saying,

"Sarry, *bahia*, [12] forgive me."

After a while the man said, "Well, can yu lend mi five rupees, ah guh pay you back soon."

"Ah noh have."

"Gad will sin yu fuh lying," the man threatened, giving the impression that he was God's chosen messenger relaying a solemn prophesy. Mattai cogitated a moment, undecided. It was not good to lie, he thought. His father had always infused that in him.

"Ah noh know yu." That was the truth, he thought, hoping that it would bring closure to the request and get rid of the stranger.

---

[11] sadhu-holy man
[12] bahia-brother

"Mi name Garibay."

Although Mattai only had a few rupees of his mother's money, he lent Garibay five of them in order to be rid of him.

Garibay left, then after a while returned puffing smoke from rolled black tobacco. He said,

"When ah get pay ah goh pay yu back," then spat on the deck carelessly.

Mattai involuntarily became an acquaintance of Garibay who confided in him, as if they were old friends, that he was a *chamar* [13] who will become a pandit in British Guiana.

"But *chamars* cannot become pandits," Mattai protested.

"Yu noh know; after yu crass *kala pani* [14] yu can become any caste, high or low. I will become a Brahmin *pandit*." [15]

"Impossible," objected Mattai, " That ah dishonesty."

"Tchu ! Yu honest?" He spat again.

No response.

"Afta yu steal rice?"

****

After what seemed like a year, the ship approached land. One day earlier, everyone had been locked below decks. Tired, weak, sickly and unkempt as they were the people hurriedly flocked by the portholes to peer outside. Everyone was curious.

---

[13] chamar- Indian of low caste
[14] kala pani- black waters
[15] pandit-pundit/Hindu priest

All they saw were a few huts next to a creek with dense trees everywhere.

"Whey we deh?"

"British Guiana!"

"Trinidad!"

"Jamaica!"

"British Honduras!"

Every one seemed to know where they were even though their answers differed. They knew that it was pointless to ask the crew who all along had been snobbish, treating them with scorn.

After a time the sails were lowered, the anchors thrown overboard and the ship was lashed with thick ropes to the dock. Finally, the gangplank was lowered. Relieved, the crowd disembarked slowly, some assisting others who were too emaciated to stand or walk on their own.

*****

INDIAN EMIGRANTS TO THE CARIBBEAN BY COUNTRY

INDIAN EMIGRANTS TO THE CARIBBEAN 1838-1917	Year First arrived	Total Emigrants
Former British Colonies		
Guyana	1838	238,909
Trinidad	1845	143,939
Jamaica	1845	37,027
St. Vincent	1856	2,472

Grenada	1857	3,200
Belize	1857	3,000
St. Lucia	1858	4,354
Former Dutch Colony		
Suriname	1873	34,304
Former Danish Colony		
St Croix	1862	321
Former French Colonies		
Martinique	1853	25,509
Guadeloupe	1854	42,326
French Guiana	1855	8,500
Total		**543,861**

OTHER COUNTRIES

Fiji	60,965
East Africa	32,000
Seychelles	6,315

3

Bonded Servant

Wearily Mattai walked back towards his home. He trudged along barefooted carrying his empty lunch tin and water bottle in a cloth bag, attached to a stick, over his left shoulder. In his right hand he held his cutlass. His tattered, one-sleeved, soot-covered shirt was glued to his back with sweat. All

Cutting Sugar Cane

day, starting at dawn, he had been cutting and stacking cane, for the most part in the sweltering sun. Day after day he had cut and carried cane. The days turned into months, then years. It had been fourteen years and his third contract since the day he arrived in this new land, British Guiana. Ever since, he had lived in Bush Lot settlement two miles from the main road in the county of Essequibo. Since his arrival, life had been one of continuous, never-ending hard work. In the beginning he fetched and stacked the cut cane. Later, as he grew older, he started

Loading iron punt with sugar cane

wielding a cutlass, cutting the cane as older men did.

After a while he stopped, put his belongings near a clump of trees and stepped amongst the knee-high grass towards the drainage canal. He paused and looked left and right scanning the grass-covered canal before him. He had marked a spot that morning by taking mental note of a particular *Jamoon* tree [1] that had a black crow on it. Now he saw several such trees but no bird on any of them.

---

[1] Jamoon tree-Blackberry tree.

Disenchanted, he looked around for a while before he found his spot. Then he reached for a bamboo rod which he had carefully hidden, walked down to the water's edge and pulled in one of his *muco-muco* [2] buoys which he had set early in the morning on the way to work. There was nothing on the fishhook which was attached to it by a one-foot string. The next one had nothing, also. He quickly became disappointed. Impatiently, he turned to fish out the third one. It felt heavy as he pulled and his mood swinged. As he lifted it both the rod and his hand shook from the tension and resistance. Lucky for him, it had a big *hurrie* .[3] He was pleased. He pulled in six more buoys and was fortunate to get two *hurries*, a large *patwa* and a *laruma* which he released back into the water because it was considered a scavenger and, thus, unclean. He carefully placed the fishes in his lunch bag, hid his bamboo rod and proceeded on his way home. Becoming

Women toiling in cane field

---

[2] muco-muco- light, succulent plant that can float easily.
[3] hurrie, patwa, laruma- fresh water fishes

elated, he began whistling his favorite *bajan* [4]. Sub-consciously, he always whistled when he was in high spirits.

Rattowa, Mattai's wife, heard his whistling from a distance and knew what to expect as if it was their secret code, their non-verbal way of communicating long distance. She too worked at the sugar estate weeding and applying manure around the 'ratoons' together with her gang members. On most days she would return home before Mattai.

This particular afternoon, as was customery, she bent barefooted on a tattered, empty rice sack in front of the clay *chula* skilfully manoeuvring a bloated *saada roti* as she balanced and rotated it with a *chimta* to ensure that it baked evenly. Af-

Sada Rotis

ter a while she lifted it by clasping it with the *chimta,* transferred it into a cloth in her other hand and dusted off the thin, almost invisible, coat of ashes with acquired proficiency. She then placed it in an empty enamel basin and covered it from a few inquisitive flies.

She peered into the Chula and, seemingly unsatisfied, reached for a *pooknie* which was tucked into the troolie overhead. She held it to her lips as if it were a flute, stooped and blew several times into the *chula*.

---

[4] bajan-religious song

The forced air rekindled the dying embers momentarily as she blew several times more. Generated smoke protested by exiting the twin surface openings, de-

Blowing fire with 'pooknie'

fying gravity as it rose, diverged mushroom-like, dissipated then converged, billowing higher and larger in a thinner mass. Sumintra coughed several times and wiped her watering eyes with the *roti* cloth. She proceeded to roll the next dough with the *belna* as Mattai entered the front door of their apartment, a part of the barrack-like *logie* [5] they occupied and, without saying anything, laid down his bag and cutlass, headed for his hammock in the corner and dropped himself in, dog-tired.

After a while, Rattowa took the bag and went through the back door to clean the fishes saying on her way out,

"Yuh food tek out. "

---

[5] logie-long, low apartment buildings for laborers.

Logie...forerunner of Townhouses

Energized by her words, Mattai quickly jumped out of the hammock, took his food, went and sat on the *perha* [6] in the kitchen and ate two *sada roties* [7] and fish curry balancing the battered enamel plate in one hand and eating with the fingers of the other. He washed it down with a cup of green tea.

Enamel Plate

He then gargled and spat before retiring back to the hammock. Almost immediately, he began to snore.

"Pa!"

He shifted and continued snoring.

"Pa!"

His daughter Rambasie, who was four, was tugging at his hammock.

"Eh."

" Pa, guess wha' ah larn in skool today?"

---

[6] perha-small, very low bench
[7] sada rotie-thick flour tortilla.

"Wha'?"

"Old McDonald had a farm."

" Wha' kinda farm, cane or rice?"

"Cane."

"McDoulan have whan farm?" he repeated drowsily. "Spell 'farm'."

"E- I- E- I- O"

He opened his eyes and turned to face her. Beaming, he hugged her around her tiny waist and said,

"Ah proud ah yu, *bettie* [8]. Whan day, yu goh be wan dakta; look after yu *pa* when eh get old."

Secretly, and intermittently, he had been a perfectionist and this made him very satisfied. It made his day.

After a while he asked,

"Weh Sook?"

Sooknanan Ghasi, called Sook, was his son.

"Ma send he to Tapa shap to buy," Rambasie replied.

---

[8] bettie-daughter

Mattai became silent. His mind shifted gears auto-matically as he started to reminisce about his errand many years ago in Calcutta; how he was lost, ac-

cused and arrested. As he thought about it, he be-came increasingly worried when night fell and the place became dark. He knew that Sook would be playing any of a number of games—'Salt', hide and seek, cricket, among others— and would not think of going home until after dark. He had scolded him on numerous occasions saying how he walked "*Nepeh, Nepeh*", indolently and slowly. Neverthe-less, he became agitated with mixed feelings of an-ger and concern and sat up, about to go outside when he heard Sook talking to Rattowa. Only then did he lie back, resting assuredly.

****

Day after day Mattai left for work before daybreak after eating and using the communal la-trine over the trench which was an open sewer. On his way he secretly threw his baited buoys into the canal at a grassy spot to conceal them. He worked very hard, always choosing 'task work' over 'day work', determined to earn the maximum wage. He chopped cane with his cutlass and stacked them. As he did, he usually overheard the sound of cane being cut by others in nearby fields, amid voices in conversation.

Not far away, other workers were constantly yelling at uncooperative oxen and mules as they hauled the long carts and iron *punts* [9] laden with cane being transported to the factory.

Mattai worked alone swinging his cutlass with great proficiency. As he did, his body was continuously covered in sweat which soaked his sparse clothing and trickled into his eyes, burning them. From time to time, he swiped his saturated forehead with the back of his left hand and shook it, shedding the invading sweat. This was done in one continuous, instinctive action that did not disrupt the rhythm of his chopping.

Mattai felt helpless; entrapped. He had never expected to work so hard in his life. However, there seemed to be no easier option, no readily available alternative. Many years before, he had stopped entertaining the thought of escaping. Then, when he was still young and restless, he had fled from his quarters and ran all night through the dark forest hoping to reach the seashore. Convinced that he could not have been that far from his homeland, he had, for many months, planned to make a raft and set sail for Calcutta. In his rush, he had thumped his right big toe, severely injuring it, on a piece of fallen bamboo. Ignoring the pain, rather enduring it, he had limped on. By daybreak, he had not reached

---

[9] punt-long rectangular metal barge/boat.

any body of water. The next day, hungry and tired, he had been caught hiding in the bushes. The Driver on horseback had taken him back to the estate. At the manager's office he had been sternly rebuked and told to pay one shilling on payday. In hindsight, he realized that he had been favored. Older men who had tried to escape had been tied to a post and severely flogged with a cat-o'-nine-tails under the manager's house. They had convulsed in pain during the ordeal which ended with salt pickle being rubbed on their wounded backs. Some of them got so ill afterwards that they had to be taken to the sick-house.

Mattai recalled visiting the sick-house to get his toe dressed. The place had been wretchedly filthy. There was an ever-present, unbearable

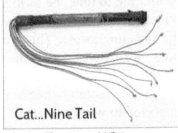

Cat...Nine Tail

Flogging Whip

odor of a mixture of Lysol disinfectant, medicine and dirt which infiltrated every room. It had made him try, unsuccessfully, to hold his breath. In every room he had seen ill people with no mattresses to lie on. They rested on dirty sheets placed on the rough wooden floor, with their wrapped clothes as pillow. In one room he had seen dead-looking people with numerous oozing sores and ulcers. The flesh of one man was rotting and the toes of another were dropping off. The stench had lingered with him even after he had left, even after he had taken a bath. Above all, the images had left a lasting impression on Mattai who, ironically, felt lucky in his dreadful condition.

Now that he was conditioned, he labored steadfastly determined to accomplish as much as possible. The pay was low, forcing him to work harder largely since he was one of the few men with a nuclear family. He was aware that other people who appealed to the magistrate about unfair wages had been turned away or ignored. To do the same would be a waste of time, futile. It was a well-known fact that the magistrates, manager and overseers were associates. They went hunting on their horses on Sundays and regularly visited each other's homes. They even visited the homes of a few workers, mostly clandestinely at nights. He considered it highly unreasonable that he, on the other hand, had to get permission to leave the estate. In his own simple analysis and evaluation he knew that the whole system was an insidious form of economic and social slavery controlled by his employers, put in place to keep some people rich at the expense of others. It had been well planned. For the likes of him, unfortunately, it meant perpetual poverty. From the time of their arrival , he realized that they were merely indentured workers. What he did not figure out, however, was that the process of deculturalization, or as some would argue, dehumanization, had begun since they left India .

Their expected gratification had been delayed for too long. It was a dead end. His ambition and dreams were changing from optimism to pessimism and, like someone wrongfully imprisoned, he longed for a change of circumstances; any change.

He was aware that life could be made easier. He knew of other men who got promoted to *Sirdar* [10] by allowing the British managers and overseers at the estate to sleep with their young unmarried daughters, even their wives. Little did he know how much this usurped privilege of *jus primae noctis*—the right of boss/king to sleep with any woman — was widespread in the colonies worldwide. He detested such men for being dishonorable and had no regard for their easily acquired status. In his own way he considered them to be sleazy opportunists, the equivalent of deceitful pimps; lazy bastards, inferior to the *harcaties* [11] who had fooled, duped and lured people away from their homeland, India. He did not even take a second glance at them or acknowledged their presence whenever their paths crossed. He had long decided that he would rather starve or die than facilitate such immoral and disgraceful deeds. Even in his state of dire need and poverty he was dignified and knew that to serve does not mean being servile—slavishly submissive—and he was determined to survive honestly.

His dislike for *Sirdars* was shared by the majority of his fellow laborers. It was common knowledge that in their privileged, intermediate status, these men who also acted as interpreters misrepresented the grievances of the workers. Worst, they did not inform the workers of the forthcoming visits of the Sub-Agents of Immigration, fearful that their complaints will be aired directly and they, the *Sirdars,* will be fired. People only knew of such vis-

---

[10] Sirdar-Driver/overseer
[11] harcatie-crook, swindler, cheat

its belatedly. At that point they would realize that they had been purposely kept in the dark, preventing them from meeting someone who they were eagerly planning to see. This forced them to suffer in silence. This was possible because they, the *Sirdars*, enjoyed some degree of immunity. Complaints of their harassment of the laborers were largely ignored by the managers who relied on them for information. Sometimes their lies resulted in the wrongful locking up of individuals in the sick-house or, worst of all, brutal flogging which was very painful and humiliating. All this only served to increase the laborers' collective hatred for them.

Mattai only stopped to rehydrate himself occasionally from his water bottle and to eat lunch which invariably consisted of boiled rice and curried vegetables with fish.

****

On Saturdays he stopped working early, by three o'clock, because he had to collect his hard-earned pay for the week. On such days, with his few belongings, he walked the three miles to the government pay office situated not far from the sugar factory. There, he usually received four shillings which he carefully placed in a cloth before knotting it. According to his own mental calculation he generally earned closer to five shillings but he would say nothing as he walked away. On one occasion when he had inquired about the amount he received, the clerk had insulted him calling him a 'stupid coolie'. As an illiterate laborer, he had few rights and, like the others, did not know how to assert himself. Appeals to the better judgment and latent humanity of the bosses in the office were not encouraged or addressed. Not giving the pay clerk the benefit of his doubts he customarily walked away angrily, feeling cheated.

On one particular day, as if to appease his disgruntlement he headed straight for Awad rum shop which was two miles away, neglecting to pick up his buoys which, he told himself, he would get later on his way home. There he joined Pagla, Talesh and Randass who were already there. The place was crowded with other cane-cutters so they sat on crates outside under a Star Apple tree enjoying a bottle of brown Russian Bear Rum.

"Wha' happen to Gadar?" he asked them.

" 'fraid a eh wife; had to go straight home," Talesh responded, chuckling.

"Real *cunu-munu* ", [12] Pagla said, downing his rum in one drink and then drinking some water.

"Eh wife gat him anda arres'," Talesh continued. They all laughed.

"Even have to get permission to use the latrine." More laughter.

Almost every adult knew that Gadar was in a matriarchal situation, controlled by his hefty wife who spared no moment to disgrace him in public. He was afraid to socialize with fellow workers; scared that she would turn up, insult him and make him leave for home in shame once again. While this was an embarrassment to Gadar, it made the rest of them, especially Talesh, feel more powerful, think-

---

[12] cunu munu- unassertive man with bossy, commanding wife.

ing of themselves as macho men. Real men were supposed to be in charge of their homes, even when they could not present their concerns and fight for their rights outside; even when they responded "Yes, bass" and " *Acha* [13] sahib" when reluctantly obeying orders at work.

It was the universal norm that even men who cooperated with their wives, in egalitarian relationships, were looked down upon by other men as being weak. Talesh, who was thin and frail, regularly bragged whenever he abused his wife physically. He told friends that Gadar's was a wimp and his wife was in control because of Gadar's softness and unassertiveness; saying that Gadar had made the mistake of letting his wife take control gradually. The solution, he was convinced, was to overreact by being abusive whenever his wife made any important decision, sometimes even if she suggested something of merit.

They continued to drink, bottle after bottle, chatting and joking, until after eleven o'clock. Then, they parted company and headed for their homes with their money considerably reduced and their spirits proportionally high. As they went, Randass staggered and Mattai walked home boldly singing, something he never did when sober. He started with a *bajan* [14], then quickly switched to other religious songs. Before he reached home he had sung a lengthy medley of over two dozen songs, including love songs, most of them sung partially

---

[13] Acha- Ok/yes
[14] bajan-religious song

while others repeatedly. At the same time, he had indirectly announced to everyone his homecoming.

Next day Rattowa shook Mattai awake. Sun had already risen and he had not gone to work.

"Yuh naah wuk tuday?"

Mattai had a terrible headache. After a while he rolled out of bed and halfheartedly left for work. On his way, he felt like throwing up as his stomach heaved from his hangover. He vowed not to drink again on his next payday.

first
sight ...
undercover

Wedding Ceremony

4

The Wedding

One day after work Rattowa told Mattai that they had been invited to the wedding of Babutty's daughter, Tara. Weddings were big events in Bush Lot settlement where they lived. In fact they were big events everywhere in the colony.

"When she gettin' marry" Mattai inquired indifferently as if that was a trivial matter. He had a way of acting casual even when he was keenly interested in something. It had benefited him on many occasions when dealing with traveling, door- to-door, salesmen who came around selling cloth and watches. It was his way of bargaining without haggling.

"De secan Sunday in June," she replied pressing her dress with a heavy flat iron she had heated on the *tawa* [1] which rested over the fire in the *chula* [2].

"Who ah de bie?"
"Ah nah know. Some whan fram Winsa [3] Castle."
There was silen ce for a while. Another mysterious encoun-

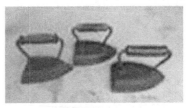

Flat Irons

ter, two complete strangers getting married, as was the custom. Mattai remembered that he had not seen Rottawa till the day of their wedding. He had wondered for weeks what she would look like. Would she be pretty? Fair? Dark? Ugly? Fat? Skinny? Deformed? It had been a time of great apprehension. He had even passed by her village several times looking at young girls and speculating which was his wife-to-be. He had not seen any particularly pretty ones but was afraid to, and unable to, cancel the wedding. Later, he realized that he had not seen her at all. He had not had so much suspense since then. Not even when his first child, his son Sook, was born. Later, he considered himself lucky as Rattowa turned out to be more beautiful— with her light brown complexion and long, black hair— than he had anticipated. He had planned to thank the

---

[1] tawa- thick, flat circular baking pan,
        called comal in some countries
[2] chula- clay fire hearth used for cooking
[3] Winsa-Windsor

Agwa [4] who negotiated on his behalf for her hand, but had never gotten around to doing so.

"Yu goin'?" Rattowa wanted to know as she exchanged the iron for another hotter one on the *tawa*.

"Weh?" His reminiscing had made him absent-minded.

"To de weddin'."

"Wha' yu mean if ah goin'? We get invite?"

It was a communal event. Everyone was supposed to be invited, not by written invitation, but verbally by a person called a *Nowa* [5]. His job was to go to each house in the village and invite the family to the wedding. In return, he collected alms—rice, coconut and so forth— from the invitees as his earnings. If, perchance, someone was not invited by mistake they would feel they were disliked by the parents of the people getting married; that they had been purposely left out and would consequently estrange themselves everlastingly, for no other

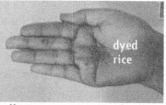

" You are invited... "

reason, from the family of the people getting married. They would never speculate that it might have been an oversight by the *Nowa*. For this reason, the *Nowa* tried his best not to omit anyone. As he delivered oral invitations he would hand them a few grains of rice, dyed yellow. Even though uninvited strangers from afar would walk in and be accom-

---

[4] Agwa-match maker.
[5] Nowa-person who relays invitations verbally.

modated at the "wedding house", an uninvited villager would never even entertain the thought of attending.

****

Three days before the wedding there was a ceremony called *"Dig Dutty"*[6]. It took place during the night. Rattowa and the children went while Mattai stayed home, satisfying himself by telling her that it was an occasion for women. Presently,

Tassa Drumming

from his bed he could hear the *tassa* [7] drums being beaten by Gocool and Lil Walker, two villagers who were considered the best drummers. The timed beating of the big bass drum in harmony with the smaller lead drum was both entertaining and disruptive to Mattai. He knew that people would be drinking, dancing and socializing. He was tempted to go out, as he was sure that some of his acquaintances would be there but decided against it, not wanting to appear as someone

Grinding Stones

---

[6] Dig-Dutty-also know as *maticore*
[7] tassa-usually a pair of drums: one small, one large.

42

who reneged on his earlier decision, a sure sign of weakness. He almost blamed himself for making the hasty decision not to go. If only Rattowa had encouraged him, just by asking once, he most likely would have been part of the "Dig Dutty" celebration. He secretly and unfairly blamed her, thinking that she was the one that did not want him to go.

On the eve of the wedding people again gathered at the venue for the wedding, a wooden house on cement pillars. It was the "Cook Night". While most of the invitees danced, drank and socialized, chosen people cooked  all night underneath the house preparing for the attendees on the following day. In an enclosed area illuminated by a Tilly gas lamp, some women were busy peeling and dicing vegetables and preparing concoctions of other ingredients, various spices, which they crushed to a puree on *massala seels*.[8]

Caharee/ cauldron and paddle

---

[8] massala seels-rubbing stones

These were sent nearby to the men who cooked them in huge *caharies* [9] along with rice and *dhal* [10] which they con-stantly stirred with long wooden paddles. All the while, there was music mixed with chat-ting, laughter and drink-ing. The cooked food was carefully stored in a makeshift room called the *bandara* [11] with one

Cast Iron Pot

man supervising its apportioning as needed. This was vital in order to minimize wastage and prevent shortage. This time, Mattai was present and actively participating by micromanaging, having been asked to take charge by the bride's father, Babutty. He moved around stirring pots, tasting, adding ingredi-ents and chatting, while at the same time giving di-rectives to others who assisted him. He was consid-ered indispensable as far as catering for large crowds were concerned, regardless of whether it was a time for celebration or sorrow. At these times his new status, from an underdog cane-cutter to a supervisor, gave him a feeling of importance and made him tireless, especially when the drinks were circulating, even though he was well aware that it was a temporary position. It was a badge of honor for him and made his days. With such feeling of self

---

[9] caharies- cauldron
s/ huge hemispherical pots
[10] dhal- cooked yellow split peas
[11] bandara-makeshift room serving as a pantry

worth, he worked unfalteringly and did not return home until the wee hours of the morning.

He was awakened the next day by a commotion in his house. It was midmorning. Rattowa and the excited children were busy getting ready to attend the wedding. He could hear a jukebox playing " Raat aur Din ...." at the wedding house which was only a stone's throw away. He got out of bed reluctantly, still groggy from the night before. He did not bother to eat since he had a hangover and no appetite. In any event, he did not expect to find cooked food in his house. As a rule, people did not cook when there was a wedding nearby. Everyone ate at the 'wedding house', consuming several meals per day. In fact, people joked about it teasing each other that they had "oiled their pots"

calabash

clay goblet

enamel cup

meaning that they put away their cooking utensils with the expectation of not having to cook for a few days, just freeloading, or rather, enjoying the generous hospitality of the hosts.

He poured some cool water from the goblet into an enamel cup and quenched his thirst, went behind the house and took a bath standing next to a drum of water and using a *calabash* [12] to douse

---

[12] calabash-half of a dried gourd used as a bowl

himself, not bothering to go to the nearby canal as he usually did.

When he reentered the house, Rattowa, Sook and Rambasie had already left. He got dressed, putting on his white, pressed long-sleeved shirt, brown serge pants, gray felt hat and stiff, black "stone crusher" shoes which he had not worn in months, saving them for special occasions.

A circuit for each vow

Marriage Vows (in a nutshell)

The Wedding

When he reached the wedding house the *Dulaha* and *Dulahin* [13] were already proceeding in circles around a sacred fire, their garment tied together, under the *maro* [14] making their seven marriage vows accompanied by the chanting of the pandit. The *maro* was well decorated with red hibiscus and other flowers, religious photos and coconut branches. Young coconuts and shiny ornaments dangled from the top.

A large crowd of people, mostly women embellished with their best clothes and bedecked with gold jewelry, was seated witnessing the ceremony. Next to them sat the smaller children who were constantly being hushed by their mothers. Men and boys were there, also, standing behind the seated guests. Some were milling around while others were chatting, inattentive to the details of the ceremony. After a while the ceremony was over and guests donated gifts in the form of cash. From where he stood Mattai could see his wife, Rattowa, presenting on behalf of the family. After a while the groom and his entourage, a procession of five donkey carts filled with *barriatas* [15] and some on foot, left for his home after being showered with rice and other confetti on their way out. There the celebration would continue all day.

Minutes later, the *tassa* [16] could be heard above all the noise. Some people gathered around it looking on; others danced. For the rest of the day

---

[13] Dulaha and Dulahin=bridegroom and bride
[14] maro-tent
[15] barriatas-groom's party
[16] tasa-drums

47

people more or less did what they wanted. The ceremony was over and they celebrated. Some danced, others drank rum while, all the time people— invited and uninvited — were fed in batches under a tent as they sat on long provisional benches and tables. Mattai went and took his place among them. A section of a banana leaf was placed in front of him. On top of it was doled out a pile of white rice. He made a depression in the middle of it with his right index finger giving it the appearance of a volcano.

"*Dhal?* " [16]

"Yes," responded Mattai.

The server poured *dhal* from a bucket using a *daboo* [17] into Mattai's model volcano until its crater overflowed.

"*Achar* ?" [18]

"Pum'kin?"

"*Baagie?* " [19]

"*Catahar?*" [20]

"*Edda?*" [21]

Each time Mattai nodded and the different courses were piled on top. It was topped off with

Serving Wedding Guests

two freshly cooked *poories*.[22] As the servers, with

---

[16] Dhal- boiled, seasoned yellow split peas
[17] daboo-ladle, dipper
[18] Achar-thick, hot, spicy sauce
[19] Baagie- dark leaf vegetable, also called callalloo
[20] Catahar-similar to Jack Fruit
[21] Edda-eddoe, root crop similar to Taro

buckets and spoons, paced up and down entreating people to have more, Mattai *sanay* [23] his food with his hand and proceeded to enjoy it. The approximately 'seven curry' he ate was particularly gratifying and he enjoyed it thoroughly, pleased with his own cooking the night before. As he ate, the *dhal* [24] ran down his raised forearm and he licked it, unmindful of anyone around.

The jukebox was now playing "Rhona Kabee Nani Rona……" and a crowd of people were dancing while others looked on. Males were dancing outside while females danced indoors. Most onlookers were focused on Dulchan, who was a very good dancer, moving in cohesion with the music, curling and uncurling both hands and even tiptoeing sometimes while moving his head rhythmically. Everyone admired him. Mattai wished he could dance as well as Dulchan. He had never taken the time to practice dancing, having been preoccupied with his work. He decided to go at the back of the house and take a drink with Pagla and Gadar who drank clandestinely as his wife socialized with the women out of sight. Later he would come back and dance, he promised himself.

---

[22] poories- thin fried flour tortillas
[23] sanay-mix with fingers
[24] dhal-cooked yellow split peas

5

Sook's Schooling

Mattai had been living in Bush Lot Settlement for over seventeen 'long' years. During all those years life had been very hard. He seemed not to be able to make material progress, ruling out his chances of attaining upward social and economic mobility. Their food was the routine vegetable with fish, rice or roti, and tea. Occasionally, they would slaughter a chicken of theirs and enjoy it. They could barely afford clothing usually going about barefooted with torn, patched clothes. Rattowa only had two dresses for special events and Mattai had one suit of good clothes. Their children fared worst with Sook going about shirtless, with patched pants, most of the time. Even though Rattowa supplemented their income by working in the weeding gang of the estate, their standard of living did not improve with two children to raise. They could not rise above the subsistence level of living. Furthermore, they were perpetually indebted to the grocer, Lall, who give them goods on credit. Mattai had a suspicion that Lall was robbing them but did not say anything because he could not prove it. Moreover, he did not want to aggravate Lall who can, at any time, cut off their source of food spitefully even if he had been ripping them off. It was déjà vu for him as he had a faint recollection that many years before his parents were in the same predicament with a mean shopkeeper in Bengal.

Very few of those who had come from India had returned as far as he knew. Many people who had arrived long before him had died penniless, as had their parents before them. As hard as they tried, they could not raise the money to pay for their return passage. Those who entertained the thought, as well as the few who had some money, were discouraged from returning and promised higher wages. They were encouraged, sometimes tricked or coerced, into signing another five-year contract. After they did, no pay increase was given. Promises and hopes became elusive dreams overtime as delusions of riches and the possibility of upliftment foreclosed. The local manager ignored their complaints and appeals and they felt helpless, victims of deceitful profiteers. Mindful of this, Mattai, unlike so many others, sent both of his children to school. He wanted them to get an education in order to put an end to poverty within the family. He wanted them to attend school and secure jobs other than fieldwork; bookkeeping or checker or office work, for instance; better yet, to become doctors or lawyers.

One day Sook came home from school with welts on his arm. He did not say anything, fearing that his father would find out that the teacher spanked him and administer a second dose without finding out if the first one was justified. Rattowa, however, spotted them because Sook usually wore no shirt at home.

"Wha' kinda maak tha'?" she wanted to know.

"Not'in."

"Not'in? Leh mi see!" She held him and examined his arm. It had about five dark, parallel ridges and was swollen.

"Who duh tha to yuh?"

"Nobaddy."

Mattai, who was resting in his hammock and who they thought had dozed off, overheard and demanded,

" Come hay bie, leh me see yu."

Sook came forward hesitantly.

Mattai held him and demanded, " Whahappen, who beet yuh?"

"Teacha."

"Which teacha?"

"De fat wan. "

"Wha' eh name?"

"Teacha Wint."

Mattai instantly became mad. He did not even thought of asking why the teacher had beaten Sook. Gnashing his teeth he snarled,

"Who ghee he de rite fu beat yuh suh baad? He want tu kill yuh? Eh want to beet *pickney* [1] eh shud meck *pickney*. Tomarra mi ah guh tu skool tu see this Mr. Wint. Ah guh show he who ah maan."

In times like these, Mattai became ballistic; he could not maintain his calm; he could not rationalize; he was not prepared to listen. No one objected to his decision or tried to change his mind realizing that he was totally infuriated, uncompromising. Even though he himself had not spared his broad, leather belt on Sook who was playful and at times disobedient to his mother, he found this to be totally unacceptable. In less serious circumstances, he would have taken his belt and whipped Sook, reinforcing the idea that the teacher must be right. This was too much for him, however. It was overkill.

Sook, on the other hand, became very frightened. This was exactly what he did not want. That night, he laid in bed for hours unable to sleep, thinking of what would happen the next day. He remembered what had happened to Rahaman, a classmate who had angered Mr. Wint before. In Scripture, Mr. Wint had informed the class that,

"God is here, there and everywhere, seeing all the bad things you all doing."

"Teacha, Gad in we kichen?" Rahaman had asked.

"Yes."

"Gad in we pig pen?" Rahaman persisted.

"Yes, everywhere!" Not accustomed to being questioned by students Mr. Wint had gotten agitated.

---

[1] pickney- child/children

"Yu lie, teacha, we noh have no pig pen, we noh mine pigs."

Rahaman had been smiling. It turned into snickering, then loud laughter. He had tricked the teacher. The rest of the class had stopped working and heard every word. Mr. Wint had become angry and, without a word, dealt several blows with his 'wild cane' to Rahaman's back. Immediately his laughter had turned into tears streaming down his agonized face. The next day Rahaman's father had taken him to see Mr. Wint. When he learned what had happened he unleashed his anger on his son, giving him a second, more severe dose with his belt in front of everyone. The thought of a similar outcome terrified Sook. He wished his father had taken him out of school before to work on the estate as some other boys did.

Early next morning Sook did not get out of bed. When called upon he complained to his mother, his face contorted, that his belly was paining. He pleaded that he did not want to go to school. Mattai became suspi-

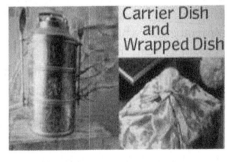

Carrier Dish and Wrapped Dish

cious. He insisted that Sook go to school as they had to go and see Mr. Wint. He had not gone to work but dressed in his better clothes—his brushed, brown felt hat, ironed, long-sleeved white shirt, brown serge pants and stiff, rarely-used, black shoes—and saw to it that Sook got dressed.

"Leh wi guh!" he commanded.

They started off walking along the brick road that led to the school. Mattai walked briskly with Sook a few paces behind struggling to keep up. His over-starched khaki shirt and short pants, without any underclothes, bruised his skin making him uncomfortable. They passed children who were also on their way to the Anna Regina Primary School. Some were leisurely playing as they made their way. Like Sook, they were all barefooted. The older ones carried their lunch dishes wrapped in cloth or stacked in shiny containers. They also had black, mostly cracked slates and tattered, dog-eared exercise books. They placed them temporarily on the ground as they amused themselves with different activities unmindful of punctuality even though they knew that Mr. Collins, the Headmaster, would be doling out lashes left, right and center at the school's entrance to all those who were tardy.

Anna Regina High Bridge

Some of them were playing with marbles, the seeds of *awaras* ,[2] as they went along while others were running, yelling, talking and laughing, or throwing

---

[2] awara- type of palm tree

55

pebbles and other objects as they played *duck and drake* in the trench.

They approached the high bridge at Anna Regina. It was a sturdy cement structure with ramps at both approaches. Many years before, it had been built by the Dutch to facilitate the passage of barges laden with sugar from the factory to the ocean and beyond. Sook looked, as if for the first time, at the swiftly flowing water as it passed under the large, raised *koker* [3] gate. On its infinite journey, it transported countless floating plants, pieces of dry sticks and debris towards the large accommodating Atlantic Ocean. Sook turned and watched as some leaves and dry sticks circled around a large whirlpool, moved closer to its center then disappeared, sucked into the undercurrent.

Anna Regina   Koker (sluice)

"Manin, Mister Mattai."

He stopped in his tracks. It was very seldom that someone referred to him as "Mister".

---

[3] koker- huge sluice gates built to regulate the flow of water

As he turned around he saw someone passing them on

Rudge Bicycle

a big-framed bicycle.

It was a stout, bespectacled Negro man in his middle age. Most teachers were descendants of slaves and were Christians, a significant requirement in order to become an educator under British colonial rule.

"Manin ," Mattai responded, then turned to Sook and asked, "Who dat?"

"Teacha Wint."

It came as a surprise that Mr. Wint knew him.

"Ah want see yu !" he yelled. Mr. Wint had already stopped and dismounted in order to push his bicycle up the remaining slope to the top of the bridge. He waited for them to catch up, his hands holdings the handlebars of his Rudge bicycle and clasping a flat, brown briefcase at the same time.

"Mr. Mattai, Sook not studying his work," he said plaintively as they approached him. His experience and survival instincts had taught him to be proactive in such encounters.

"Nah study?" Mattai turned to Sook who bowed as if in prayer.

"He not studying Scripture," Mr. Wint continued, "I asked him who wanted to stone the wicked woman, and you know what he said?"

"Wha'? "

"He said that he was absent from school; he did not want to pelt any woman."

"Eh right," Mattai said defensively, " Eh bin ah farm wid mi laas week."

"John, chapter eight, verse seven, Mr. Mattai; who wanted to stone the adulterous woman? Sook has to study religion."

"But yu beat this bie fu nutten, fu nutten at all," Mattai   retorted angrily, as if he had not heard Mr. Wint's answer.

Mr. Wint stood speechless, unsure of what to say next; uncertain of whether he would appease Mattai or add fuel to fire.

There was a brief, uncompromising silence. Then, without further ado, Mattai snapped,

"Leh we guh home, bie," trembling with rage and ushering Sook towards home. As they moved away, he continued,

"Yu shore yu na stone de lady?"

"No pa."

"Yu see anybaddy pelt she?"

"No."

****

After that Sook did not return to school. Secretly, Mattai wanted him to get an education but he did not insist when Sook complained that he did not want to go back to school. In fact, Sook had *skulked* [4] from school on several occasions when he and two friends had gone into the bushes shooting birds with their sling shots. Those had been great times as they salted and roasted doves and other birds on an open fire, swam in the canal for hours and ate mangoes, guavas, papayas and other fruits, always careful not to be seen. He liked being out of school more than attending.

Sook started to go the cane field with him and helped in fetching and stacking the cane which he cut. Thus his education became informal training. Overtime he learned how to cut cane, catch fishes with buoys and cultivate vegetables in the patch beside their home. To him this was an achievement, a right of passage to manhood. He no longer considered himself a small boy. In time, they bought a cow from Husman with money Rattowa had covertly saved in a tin can through her thriftiness, budgeting and sacrifice. Sook took care of the cow, taking it to graze and water and, after it gave birth, milking it.

Educating Sook formally was never mentioned again.

---

[4] skulk-play hooky/shirk

6

Phagwah

Years of subsistence living came and passed and Mattai, along with many others of his ilk, struggled unendingly to survive. Feelings of nostalgia for his past life, his parents, younger brother and sister faded overtime. Now and then his thoughts roamed and he speculated about them. Would his parents be alive? If so, are they well? Are his brother Gobin and his sister Chandra married? Does he have nieces and nephews? Did they get the message he had sent with Ballyram who went back to Calcutta many years ago? There were always more questions than an-

Flambeau / bamchodie

swers. Newly arrived people from India did not know any of his family members.

The sugar industry at Bush Lot settlement had closed down as indentureship came to an end in the 1920's due to the determined, unwavering efforts of Mohandas "Mahatma" Gandhi and others who learned about the abuse and exploitation of their countrymen overseas. After completing three five-year contracts, Mattai was now a free peasant farmer. Like many others, he leased eight acres of land by the local authorities to cultivate rice. Henceforth, material progress was slow. For a time his family lived in a 'Watch House' beside his field sharing it with unwelcomed rats, bugs, houseflies and ants. It was thatched with a *troolie* palm roof, had mud-plastered, windowless, wattled walls and an earthen floor which Rattowa daubed industriously with a watery blend of clay and cow's dung. Two used rice bags hung in the doorway in place of a door. At nights the dark, chilly interior was lighted by a homemade, unshaded *bamchodie* [5] whose

Wattle and thatch huts

[5] bamchodie-flambeau/bottle lamp

flickering light choreographed the movement of surrounding shadows. The paradise that some people were told about to encourage them to leave India turned out to be a carrot in front of a donkey, nothing more than a bait.

They lived, barely managing to survive, for four years in this humble abode. By sheer hard work of his family members, the income from his rice field and selling three oxen to a butcher, not to mention the thriftiness and frugality of Rattowa, he built a small wooden house not far from his field. Unlike their previous abode, it was covered with corrugated zinc sheets, had an uneven, creased wooden floor and a small porch surrounded by latticework. At nights, it was illuminated by a shaded hurricane lantern, which Rattowa carefully wiped, filled with kerosene oil and lighted. As soon as he received cash for his rice crop, Mattai replaced it with a shiny Petromax gas lamp which he himself pumped and lighted ritually every evening, not wanting it to be touched by anyone else. This move manifested his progress as many others were still living in cramped *logies* [6] next to obnoxious cesspools under communal latrines. Also, many more still lived in thatched 'watch houses' which were infested with rats and roaches and leaked profusely when it rained. Sook was now a young man of sixteen and his daughter Ramba-

Gas Lamp

---

[6] logies-long, low , barrack-like, apartment buildings

sie, who had stopped going to school since she was eight, had married three years before at age fifteen. She had gone to live at her husband parents' house in Philadelphia, far away across the Essequibo River. In fact, he and Rattowa had become grandparents two years after. They had traveled by cart and boat all the way to Philadelphia to celebrate the ninth day of the child's birth and take gifts, as was customary. They returned as proud maternal grandparents—*Nana* and *Nani* [7]— of a baby girl so beautiful that they nicknamed her Rosie while her official name was Leila.

They did not do much work on Sundays. In the mornings they went to the *Mandir* [8] to worship. Mattai was entering middle age and was becoming mellow. He only drank socially now and took religion seriously.

"Wat a man sow he guh reap," he told Sook one day as they sat on their back stairs watching a game of cricket in progress on an adjacent grassy field made bumpy by cattle tracks. One batsman had hit the ball and it was being desperately chased by a fielder while the batsmen ran frantically, passing each other, trying to score more runs.

"Wat about them who thief?" Sook asked, "They plant wha' they thief?"

"Yu nah andastan," he retorted, "Yu too young to andastan life."

Sook got up and ran a few yards towards a ball that had passed the boundary line coming towards them.

---

[7] Nana-maternal grandfather; Nani- maternal grandmother
[8] Mandir- temple

It bumped into a fallen block of firewood, ascended a few feet and he intercepted it as if, anticipating its flight, he had waited for this moment. He threw it with great force onto the field to no one in particular.

"Mi andastan," he replied, "If yu sow rice, yu reap rice."

Taking things literally, Sook did not want to be outdone. By then the spectators, mostly men, who had been drinking were jubilant. They were cheering and some were shouting advice and encouragement to both batsmen who could not hear them above the noise. The batsmen were from the home team. At that point, unfortunately, one of them was bowled by a fast bowler who hit his 'stumps' sending one flying a few yards. Spectators, even those who backed the home team, ran on to the field temporarily interrupting the game, surrounded the bowler and attempted to shake his hands. One of them had a bottle and glass trying to give him a congratulatory drink. It took about five minutes for order to be restored, after which the game continued.

Mattai did not pursue the topic of cause and corresponding effect further. Even though he was illiterate, he was intelligent enough to know that it is folly to be wise in certain situations. In time, Sook would get a better grasp of life, he surmised, as age brings wisdom.

****

Mattai became progressively religious with each passing year. He believed in the Laws of Karma: that ones deeds determine their destiny. Thus, he wanted to live a good life. Unfortunately, he failed to impress this upon his son, Sook. This law, together with his strong belief in reincarnation caused him to accept and resign himself to his condition in life. It made life more tolerable, more livable. Though he did not know it, millions of people held the same beliefs. They collectively felt that if they were poor and suffering, it was because of their deeds— rather misdeeds— in their former lives. On the contrary, those who were wealthy and living in luxury must have been good in their previous life. It was simply cause and corresponding effect: very simple, very pragmatic. This resulted in the strong resolve to live honest, hardworking, God-fearing lives by some of them. It did not matter what other people did; that was their business. No one attempted to reform or convert them. The Law of Karma would take its course.

Mattai became more active at the *Mandir*. He did not miss any function, chanted verses from the Ramayana daily and availed himself for voluntary communal activities such as weeding, digging and building. His faith caused him to look forward to religious seasons such as Phagwah [9] a period of thanksgiving when Hindus, by tradition, celebrated the coming of spring and the triumph of good over evil. During this time he skipped work and went around with the *Chowtal* [10] group singing and clapping his pair of *gaal*. [11] Dressed in white, they would visit various homes for days and entertain the

---

[9] Phagwah- also called Holi
[10] Chowtal-religious song
[11] gaal- small pair of cymbals

hosts by chanting and singing, beating a *dolak* [12] and making music with their *dhantal* [13] and *gaal*. In return they were given drinks

and lots of food— *channa* [14], *polourie, bara, prasad, keer* [15], *and* so forth— at each house they visited.

Burning Holika

The highlight during this period was the burning of the *Holika* [16] on the eve of Phagwah and the celebration that followed. All day, merry makers went around dousing people with *abeer* [17] and powder and there was continuous eating and drinking. Whole communities were involved, Muslims and Christians as well, though some participated reluctantly, passively and involuntarily. In the end, the whole affair lasted about two weeks and Mattai was both filled and fulfilled. This annual celebration as well as *Diwali, Eid* [18] Christmas and Easter were times of happiness which punctuated the life of drudgery of the ex-

---

[12] dolak- hand drum slung around the neck.
[13] dhantal-percussion instrument comprising of short steel rods.
[14] channa- chick peas/ garabanso beans
[15] polourie, bara, prasad, keer-various delicacies/fingerfoods/sweetmeats
[16] Holika-huge bonfire with religious significance
[17] abeer- a red liquid made by mixing a powdery substance with water.
[18] Diwali,Eid- Hindu and Muslim religious holiday respectively.

indentured servants. They cushioned hard times and made life in general more worthwhile.

Celebrating Phagwah

Police Station and Magistrate Court

7

Swift 'Justice'

Mattai slowly approached the police station in Anna Regina. It was a large, three-storied, colonial style, wooden building which also housed the Magistrate's Court. He progressively became nervous as he came closer with his heart beating faster. He felt like turning back, running away, and disappearing. As far back as he could remember, he was always uncomfortable in formal procedures, where he had little say and no control over events or time frame. Owing to this, he had always kept away from public buildings especially government ones. These buildings were always full with tons of books and huge tables occupied by scholarly, well-dressed men. They usually carried stuffed brief cases, smoked pipes casually and were bespectacled, symbols of learning and education. This made Mattai uneasy in their presence. If, in addition, they were bearded, the ultimate badge of knowledge and wisdom, he avoided them totally, feeling that they had some authority to seal his fate even if he unintentionally upset them. He had heard that such men did not even have time to shave so preoccupied were they studying their books. He wondered with awe how these men could remember all the things in a thick book, much less a whole set of them. Only the thought that several angry policemen would come looking for him with sticks and handcuffs kept him going towards the courthouse.

He stopped at the small bridge leading to the compound and surveyed the situation. Several groups of people were already in the compound waiting, all dressed with their good clothes, some with shoes. He approached hesitantly. As he got closer the odor of coconut oil became stronger. All the laborers, including himself, used it as hair tonic and skin ointment. Some even wiped their leather shoes with it. He crossed the bridge and nodded to Talesh who stood with another group of people, including his wife Kumarie. Her presence surprised Mattai as, urged by another woman, she had reported to the police that Talesh had beaten her. As a result, he had had been charged with assault and battery. Mattai could not figure why they were there together chatting as if nothing had happened.

Presently, the braying of a donkey, followed by another which added several successive loud snorts, caught Mattai's attention. He turned and saw a wooden corral full of impounded animals, mainly oxen, donkeys and sheep in the far corner of the compound. Curiously, he stepped closer to get a better look taking care not to go too near and break another law. There among them he saw his missing black and white bull, the source of his summons to attend court. As he stood watching, there was the honking of a horn, which sounded several times, indicating impatience.

All heads turned to see a large black Triumph car, with a small Union Jack fluttering on its *bonnet,* [1] crossing the bridge and entering the compound. It drove right up to the main entrance of the police station and stopped. People who were sitting around talking stopped and stood up. They knew that the newcomers were people of importance as no one else was entitled to toot horns or make noise near the police station which was strictly a silent zone because it housed the Magistrates' Courts. Instantly, the middle-aged Negro driver came out and opened the back doors, one at a time, to facilitate the exit of two White men who looked like opposites: one was tall and thin, the other short and overweight; one bearded, the other cleanly shaven. As if extending the difference on purpose, only one of them smoked a pipe which had a pleasurable aroma while the other wore silver framed spectacles. Apart from that, both of them were dressed in

---

[1] bonnet- British term for hood of car.

suits and carried crammed black briefcases. Such deportment to the ordinary people meant power, knowledge and authority. They looked straight ahead, ignoring everyone, as they stepped forward through the large double doors where a policeman briskly saluted them. Mattai was not sure who they were but knew that they had to be men of great importance from their appearance and dress and the treatment and reception they received. Chauffeurs did not usually open doors for passengers and the police had always been callous and unapproachable to lesser beings of no significance.

Mattai was mystified by their deference. He wondered if such men ever walked barefooted, joked or gossiped. Can they swim? Do they drink alcohol or dance? Go fishing? Eat with their bare hands or wear ordinary clothes at home? He had never seen them at a wedding or funeral or anywhere else and their existence was an unsolved mystery to him. His train of thoughts was broken by the shuffling as people began to enter the building by a smaller side door. He followed them up a narrow flight of stairs into a large room with long parallel wooden benches. They looked exactly like the ones he had glimpsed people sitting on in a Christian church in Henrietta, the neighboring village.

They all sat and, before long, were ordered to stand by a police who yelled,
"Court rise!" As they stood reverently, the tall man who had emerged from the car minutes earlier strolled in and sat behind a large table facing them. He must be the magistrate. Even though he did not

71

know any of the two men, Mattai felt relieved that he was not the bearded one who smoked the pipe.

They were told to sit and almost immediately were called, individually, by a policeman who mispronounced many of their names causing confusion, embarrassment and delays. As each timidly came forward and stood, hat in hand, charges against them were read by the magistrate who shuffled through a stack of papers.

Offenses covered a wide continuum of infractions: public drunkenness and disorderly conduct, larceny, praedial larceny, assault, not paying their debt to Lall and other shopkeepers, their cattle damaging property or crops, fighting over the few women available and battering the ones they married. The magistrate dispensed with them quickly. A sure sign of his book learning, Mattai decided. Fines also covered a wide range: from fifty cents to five dollars. Mattai had to pay one dollar for being 'careless and allowing' his oxen to graze a portion of another farmer's rice crop. He wanted to explain that his oxen was securely tied, that he was sure that someone taken it to be impounded just for the bounty. Instead, he stood dumbfounded, unable to utter a single word, wondering whether the magistrate spoke only perfect English. If so, would he understand his explanation?

Out of curiosity and because of friendship he remained in court to hear the case against Talesh, which was left for last due to its serious nature.
After the charges were read, the magistrate asked, "How do you plead—Guilty or not guilty?"

"Nat guilty, bass," Talesh, hat in hand with shirt neatly tucked in, answered. He was unusually bold considering the seriousness of the accusation.

"Say 'your honor,'" the police officer coached.

"Nat, guilty, sahib, mi honna," Talesh said.

"Not 'my honor', ' your honor,'" the police corrected. Talesh stood speechless, confused.

The policeman approached him and, after some explanation, Talesh nodded.

"What is your address?" the magistrate continued, after writing in his book.

"Wha bass?"

"Where do you live?"

"Near Sudeen."

"And where does Sudeen live?"

"Between mee and Ramclam, mi honor," Talesh explained giving the relative location of his residence. This did not satisfy the court so after another pause his specific location, his address, was determined and noted.

Belna and Chowkey

"Why did you assault Kumarie?"

"Mi only defend miself, bass, you honna, she attak mi with the *belna* [2] furst." The magistrate, obviously puzzled, looked at Talesh inquiringly his head tilted at an angle. Talesh misunderstood his body language. Thinking that he was making a good impression and representing himself well, he stared

---

[2] belna-rolling pin

back confidently waiting for the next question. There was complete silence. Talesh, cocky as ever and full of himself, then turned around and looked at the sparse, all-male audience which he assumed were on his side. It ended when the policeman approached the magistrate and gesticulated as he spoke. The magistrate threw back his head, laughed then looked at the prosecutor who, as if on cue, joined him. The policeman smiled. Everyone else remained emotionless, unsure whether it was appropriate or permissible for them to publicly exhibit delight under such gloomy circumstances.

To present their case, the prosecutor, the fat, bearded man who had arrived with the magistrate called Kumarie to testify. She contradicted Talesh at first saying that he was drunk and hit her several times with his fist for no reason. She went on, answering further questions and, obviously confused changed her story saying that she did wave her *belna* provokingly at him.

The magistrate called for eyewitnesses. The prosecutor looked around, then spoke quietly with Kumarie. There was none. He decided to give Kumarie the benefit of the doubt since she was bruised and fined Talesh five dollars. It was not the maximum for battery but because of the mitigating circumstance of being provoked, he considered it justified. Talesh, however, felt wronged and started to threaten Kumarie as soon as they stepped outside. She fearlessly and loudly responded, gesticulating and insulting him as they went along, dispelling his earlier, frequent declarations of being the all-powerful domestic dictator.

Mattai was disgruntled for other reasons. He felt that the system was geared to penalize the poor peasants by taking back money they had saved through extreme sacrifice, from the pittance they earned. It was just a way to put them in their place; not really intended to serve justice. He was convinced that there was miscommunication between the magistrate and the accused people. In his case, there was no communication. The person to help explain, the *Dougla* [3] interpreter, had not been in court that day. This, he felt, had resulted in prejudice to so many poor people. It was a travesty of justice. Or was it? It was rumored that the interpreter sometimes misrepresented the facts when converting Hindi and patois into English and even took sides, getting kickbacks discreetly. Mattai did not know whether his, the interpreter's, presence would have helped or harmed his case and made any difference in the penalty. As he analyzed the events, his bewilderment for these learned men increased. Did the magistrate ever plant trees or keep any animal, even a dog he wondered. Did he have a wife and children?

As he drove his released cattle home, well dressed and incongruent behind it, he vowed to get back at the person who had impounded it.

---

[3] Dougla- biracial mixture of East Indian and Black/Creole.

75

8

Rice-The Bread of Life

Mattai's life revolved around his rice field, cattle, family and religion. He was always occupied. Routinely, he would rise before sunrise. After pray-ing, he would walk a mile and a half to milk his two cows. On his way back he would always have his *Black Sage* [3] in his

Ploughing rice field with wooden plough

---

[3] Black Sage- plant whose stem is used for brushing teeth

mouth and his aluminum can full of fresh milk. His breakfast was usually *sada roti* [4] with vegetable which was reaped from his garden and Red Rose, sometimes Fever Grass, tea with milk from his cows. Between eight and nine o'clock he would start out again for his rice field with his packed lunch, this time accompanied by Sook.

Rice was the staple diet of the villagers. At least twice per day—midday and evening—families ate rice. White or

Raking Field

brown 'parboiled' rice was eaten with vegetables, fish or chicken which were always referred to as 'curry' regardless of whether they were fried, stewed or curried. Domesticated animals that were not herbivorous, such as cats, dogs and chickens were also fed rice. In the fields there was always work associated with rice cultivation to be done.

This was so because rice cultivation was very labor intensive. As a

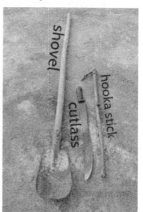
Farming Tools

---

[4] sada roti-thick flour tortilla

result, people were kept busy plowing with yoked pairs of oxen, weeding, digging, transplanting, regulating water by irrigating and draining, and keeping away birds and pests from the rice paddies. Because of the variety of tasks, light and strenuous, most family members were involved daily.

All this culminated in harvesting, transporting and selling the paddy at the huge factory with its majestic brick chimney at Anna Regina.

Placing beeya/seedlings for transplanting

Transplanting Rice Seedlings(planting rice)

Rain did not deter Mattai and he seemed immune from cold, flu and fever which affected others. He could not understand why some farmers stayed at home and neglected their fields, allowing them to be overrun by weeds. He considered them to be lazy and used to tell Sook,

"Them people really *corehee*.[5] *Coreheness* nah gat no cure."

It was his way of instilling proper work ethics in Sook who hardly ever digested what he was saying, more occupied with practical, trivial things. Sometimes Rattowa accompanied them, but mostly she stayed at home engaged full time as she washed, cooked, tended the vegetable garden and raised poultry. Nevertheless, her presence was particularly needed during the harvesting of the rice paddies. The three of them would spend all day cutting the rice stacks with curved 'grass knives'.[6] Bending, they grabbed clumps of rice plant with their left hands and cut them with their knives which they held in their right hands. They placed the cut wads in piles. It was hard, backbreaking work and the sun was always extremely, unbearably hot but they persevered without protesting. Who would they complain to?

---

[5] corehee- lazy, ackward
[6] grass knife- sickle

Cutting rice with grass knife (inset)

Threshing paddy manually

On most days Rattowa would leave for home at about four not because she was excused from the hard work but due to the fact that she had to cook dinner and do other chores. Mattai and Sook would continue working. They would harness their pair of oxen with a *juat* [7]which they then attached with ropes to a *slide* [8]. Then they would drive them out to the fields to bring in   the sheaves of rice after loading them unto the *slide.* In this way they brought in the harvest as together they transported the rice paddies, still on the stack, and piled them neatly in the *Watch House.* By then it would be long after nightfall and they would head for home, fatigued.

In times like these, Mattai had mixed feelings about the fact that he had not sent Sook back to school after his encounter with Mr. Wint. On the one hand, he was getting much needed help from Sook and, on the other, without an education Sook would be condemned to a life of struggles and hard work. His religious creed and philosophy always allayed his feelings of ambivalence, however, as he believed strongly that a person was in their present situation because of divine providence; because of karma; that one's condition was predestined by God and no other course in life was possible. Making

[7] juat-wooden yoke
[8] slide- wooden boat-like sled pulled by oxen

poor or good choices did not matter since all choices were controlled by a divine, superior being. Nevertheless, he did not communicate his feelings to anyone, fearing that evaluating his past decision openly may be looked upon as a sign of weakness and lack of certainty.

Sometimes they got help. Rambasie and her husband, Seebarran, would come from way over the Essequibo River to assist them. Those were good times as the family reunion helped to alleviate the agony of hard manual labor. At nights and at work during the day, they would constantly chitchat, filling in the others with occurrences in their lives and happenings over the past year. One night, Rattowa related about the time she had witnessed Talesh chasing Sadoo. Around ten in the morning, she had been busy washing clothes on the *staling* [9] by the trench when her attention was caught by two figures speedily approaching on the adjacent dam. She recognized Sadoo as he galloped pass, just a few yards away, with surprising swiftness for his overweight, over two hundred fifty pounds. Minutes later, Talesh with a raised cutlass in hand, gritting his teeth and cursing rushed pass in hot pursuit. Talesh, who was slender and agile, was catching up. Suddenly, to her surprise, Sadoo rushed down the slope and leaped into the canal where he submerged with a splash. His enormous weight caused huge concentric waves to swash the canal sides washing her bar of soap into the water. Talesh just stood on the bank watching. After about two minutes, Sadoo emerged

---

[9] staling-stepped, wooden structure at canal side /small dock

near the other side and clambered up with great difficulty after being bogged down and stuck in the semi-solid mud. There he stood dripping on the other bank in one shoe, his chest heaving. Only then did he look back for his attacker. Talesh stood on the other side, brandishing his cutlass and shouting, "Yuh lazy, sonovabitch, ah guh kill yu nex time!"

They all laughed as she described the event.

Anna Regina Rice Factory

pitchfork

Threshing Rice

They could not figure why Talesh had not pursued Sadoo further and did not know why he was chasing him in the first place. They changed topics and talked of other scenarios. Those were bittersweet times, comic relief from hard labor.Mattai's daughter and son-in-law could not be there every harvest as they had both a rice and cane farm of their own to attend to. During their absence, Mattai, Sook and Rattowa worked late into the nights mostly in the 'watch house' with the light of a *bamchodie* [10]. One night, Sook was walking, pitchfork in hand, behind

Paddy

the oxen in circles around a post mashing a pile of rice to separate the

separating chaff from grains

Winnowing Paddy

grains from the stack. Mattai was occupied nearby. They had not spoken for a while so absorbed were they with their work and thoughts. Suddenly, without forewarning, Sook said,

"Pa, ah whant fuh be wan police."

---

[10] bamchodie- flambeau, bottle lamp

"Wha' yu seh bie?"

Mattai, who was putting threshed paddy into jute bags, did not hear him.

"Ah want to be wan policeman."

Mattai stopped working and let go of the bag which fell, spilling some of the grains. Rattowa had remained later than usual because of the demanding work. In the moonlight outside, she was out of earshot winnowing the paddy in a huge sieve hanging on a frame in order to separate the grains from the chaff. Hence, she was unable hear Sook's request.

" But ah wha' yu want to be whan police haffica fah, yu na dey hay good?" he asked, taken aback.

"Ah want fuh deh betta, ah want stap ricefield wuk and wuk fuh salary."

"Yuh mad or wha'?"

Household chores included sifting rice and grating coconut:

Mattai was getting visibly agitated. He did not say anything more. With more gusto than before, he picked up the bag, shook it energetically with both hands and patted the sides. Then he started stitching it close using a long, black needle. Sook, dreading disapproval, did not press the issue

That night he told Rattowa, as she sat sifting rice , of Sook's ambition. She laughed, feeling that it was only wishful thinking by Sook and he would soon change his mind. Later, as Mattai lay in his bed, he could not help thinking about the implications of Sook's interest. He had a secret respect, almost fear of policemen since his boyhood days in Kolkota. At the same time, he knew of the prestige his son would bring to the family as a policeman. He could almost see people referring to him as "Consable Sook pa" or "Tha' police fada". His opinion vacillated as he did not know what to make of it. Subsequently, with the influence of Rattowa who had herself been swayed by Sook, he agreed reluctantly to his son becoming a police officer.

Sook had to take an interview which he assured Mattai would be very easy. Baldeo, a young policeman who had recently come to live in the village of Cotton Field had told him it was not difficult.

"Only t'ree questans you have to ansa," Baldeo had said calmly.

Baldeo commanded much respect and admiration because he freely told everyone he came in contact with that he had gone to a private high school. He promptly informed them that he had spent seven years at Queen's College. That was in Georgetown, the capital, a place where few people from Sook's community had gone. In fact, Sook did not know anyone personally who had gone to Georgetown. Besides, seven years at high school was a long time. The word had circulated like wildfire. Over a short time everyone knew of this either by way of gossip or by Baldeo himself. They also became aware that he had actually spent two years more than another young man who attended another high school. Everyone was impressed.

"Only t'ree questans?" Sook had been surprised.

"Yes," Baldeo had continued conspiratorially as he lowered his voice to a whisper, "and all yuh gat fuh seh is '22, 18 and both'." He had looked around cautiously as if scared of being overheard revealing confidential state secret, tantamount to committing treason.

Sook was very glad for such unsolicited help coming so generously. He knew that Baldeo was a good, respected policeman who wanted to help him.

Morris Oxford

9

The Interview

On the day of the interview Mattai did not go to work. He felt that it was his duty to give his son moral support. After milking his cows he got dressed and accompanied Sook to the Anna Regina Police Station. This time, he was not fearful about going to the police station. In fact, he was as anxious as Sook who had barely slept the night before spending time to polish his shoes to a shine, hoping to impress the interviewers.

At they walked along the earthen road, alongside the canal, Sook muttered, " 22, 18,both."

"Wha'?"

"Not'ing."

The Interview

Silently Mattai prayed along the way as he did when something was urgently desired. He continued with greater frequency as they approached their destination, avoiding the stares of people he would normally hail. He did not want to confide in anyone the nature of their mission, to let them know that Sook was going to be a police, preferring to surprise them later.

When they reached the police station, Mattai stayed under a huge Silk Cotton tree outside and Sook proceeded up to the second storey where a group of young men were already waiting. Sook scrutinized them. They were of different races: mostly of African descent, of Asian descent like himself, with one Amerindian and a few mixed.

As he sat on a bench next to an immaculately dressed, robust young man Sook's courage gradually started to evaporate and he unexpectedly became timid, temporarily loosing his enthusiasm. His feeling deepened as he looked around. Like his father and all poor peasant farmers he was not accustomed to dressing formally and going to public places. The presence of so many confident looking men chatting and joking, with all the police officers moving around, intimidated him and he felt ill at ease. As hard as he tried, he could not regain his composure. After a while, however, he became conscious that he had an advantage over the others. He knew the answers to the forthcoming questions, thanks to officer Baldeo. This unfair advantage consoled him and, feeling better, he smiled

After a while names began to be called and people from his group went individually into a room. In roughly five minutes each emerged and went outside to rejoin their relatives and friends. Since the expression in their faces did not reveal any clue of their fate, it was impossible to tell which ones were selected and which were not. Perhaps they did not know as yet.

"Sooknarine, " a voice called out loudly.

Sook jumped up instinctively from his seat, then realizing it was not his name sat back awkwardly. From the conversation around him he gathered that it was someone else being arraigned in Magistrates' Court in another part of the building.

As he waited, he imagined himself dressed in his police uniform, his hair cut short and his shoes gleaming. As he walk along the street grown people older than himself would respect and admire him and children would hide, fearing his authority and power as he had hidden from police in his younger days, even when they had done nothing wrong. He would even get opportunities to escort prisoners to Georgetown for trial at the Supreme Court.

"Sooknanan Ghasi!"

He rose from the bench and proceeded toward the large room. Inside there was one White and two Black policemen sitting in front of a huge desk covered with papers. From the decorations and stripes on their shirts, especially the White one, he knew that they were high ranking. This made him uneasy once again.

"Sit down, we have a few questions to ask you," the most decorated White one, who seemed to be the leader, said.

"What is your Height?" the other police asked.

Sook almost blurted out "22", but caught himself quickly, realizing that it could not be the correct answer. He almost panicked. He could feel the heavy palpitation of his heart. Instead, he replied,

"Five feet , seven inches."

"Five seven," the one in the middle repeated as he wrote in his notebook. Sook felt a little better.

"How many years of education do you have?"

"22"

"22! You can't be serious," another one yelled.

They looked at each other in shock, one of them rolling his eyes and resting his pen on the desk. A moment of silence, which seemed like minutes to Sook, followed. He became jumpy again, more ill at ease. By then he could not remember what they had asked him so he could not correct any possible mistake. He shifted in his seat and felt sweat trickling down his back.

He tried to remember his prepared answers. Was it '22, 18 and both'?

"OK scholar, what is your age?"

"18." The words hardly came out, almost a whisper. Sook felt his belly griping and wanted to use the toilet but could not leave, trapped in a place far removed from his comfort zone.

The officers looked at each other speechless then at Sook. Sook felt he was making progress, sat up straight and braced himself for the next question.

"Our time is limited," the leader said, "Do you honestly think that we have time to waste or we don't have better things to do?" It was a rhetorical question, requiring no answer.

"Both, Sir!" Sook ejaculated, grasping his chance.

One of the officers laughed loudly while the other two were emotionless.

The laughing policeman stopped suddenly and snapped, " We can't accept you."

"We do not want more idiots in the police force," the other one said.

"Twenty-two years of schooling," the third one mocked as Sook walked out, puzzled.

He could not understand what had happened towards the end of the interview. He could not figure out what went wrong. Is this because of his race? Or was it because he said "Both, Sir?" Should he have said "Both, Officer" instead? "Both Sahib?" Had they not seen his brightly shining shoes or paid attention to his appearance and clothes?

While waiting Mattai had arranged one of the few taxicabs available, a huge gray Riley car for their ride back home. It was the first time Sook traveled by car. He sat erect in the front seat, next to the driver, his face close to the windshield with his nose practically plastered to it, wondering how the driver kept the car on the road without seeing the wheels. As he looked outside donkey carts and cyclists they passed seemed to be marking time, even moving backwards. Mattai, in the back seat, waived

at people he had earlier avoided, people who now did not recognize him.

As they proceeded homeward he asked, " You pass?"

"Ah na know yet, they guh leh we know later," Sook lied.

The following year Sook once again took the interview to become a police. This time he passed it, but failed the physical. He was actually five feet, six and three quarters inches tall and the minimum height required was five feet seven inches. Once again, he felt discriminated against as repeated measurements by himself showed that he was tall enough. Henceforth, he gave up all aspirations of becoming a policeman, since his days of getting taller were over. He remained a rice farmer for the greater part of his life.

Labourers' Houses

10

Vicissitudes of Life

In his nineteenth year Sook got married. For the most part, it was in response to Rattowa's constant complaint of being tired, working too much and needing to rest her 'tired' bones'. His marriage, like that of his parents, was arranged. Like his parents too he and his wife got closer after marriage and developed an unexpressed love for each other. The family grew from a nuclear to an extended one. The house was also extended with the addition of another   room.

The wedding was a grand affair. Jukebox, *tassa*, [1] and a band were hired to play. Coosa was there from beginning to end, celebrating. He had walked all the way from Mainstay to be there, with his newly acquired shoes tied by the laces and slung over his neck for their protection and his packed grip.

Grip

As he sat down lacing them, he was asked about the whereabouts of Gadar who lived closer, in Cotton Field. He, without delay, said that Gadar's wife had not given him permission to come and had only recently beaten him up. However, people did not take Coosa seriously. Perhaps he was saying this to indirectly proclaim his make-belief machismo. He had told so many jokes and lies that he had lost all credibility. People did not know when he was telling the truth. He himself did not think he was scandalous and sought attention by constantly fabricating tales.

In the end Coosa stayed after the last group, who were close relatives of Sook, had departed. He embedded himself comfortably, oblivious that he was overspending his time as a guest and not feeling awkward or embarrassed at all. After eating he would 'throw back' in a hammock made of rice

---

[1] tassa-drums

sack, lethargic from a sugar high due to insufficient insulin in his system and inactivity. Like a *Cammudie* [2] immobilized as it digested an oversized prey, he rested. Only his mouth yapped on. He repeatedly thanked them for their generosity saying 'God bless you', praised their progress and compared them with less fortunate families to underscore his point. Not even when the quality of food diminished, a tangible indicator to most people that it was time to leave, did he leave. For Coosa, happiness meant getting things free, whether it was food or accommodation, preferably both. Day after day he sat chatting and chewing. He would not allow any left over food to be dumped, choosing to consume it himself. He would scold all 'offenders' by saying sternly that,

"Willful waste cause willful want ". He reinforced this by relating how penniless families, families he knew personally, had been well-to-do in the past but prodigal, the genesis of their poverty.

Believing in division of labor by gender, he would leave the empty utensils wherever he ate, knowing that Sumintra would clear them away. Instead, he would lie in the hammock clap and rub his extended abdomen and emphasize that he had to " Stop *rashin* [3] from spoil" as if he had been officially mandated to prevent wastage of food on earth. He thought that he was doing a service and never lifted a finger to be of assistance. However, he kept the family lively with many tales and informed them

---

[2] Cammudie:Boa Constrictor-large snake that wraps and squeezes its victim, then consumes it.
[3] rashin- ration/ food

that he had to attend another wedding soon in Aberdeen.

In the end, he excused himself and left. His unexpected departure took place when Sook went briefly to milk his cows and Sumintra asked him for assistance in splitting some firewood. He did not remember division of labor by gender then. He simply packed his grip, slung his shoes around his neck and walked away, sidestepping the sharp, furnace-baked, clay bricks on the road.

****

Sook's wife Sumintra was very industrious and relieved Rattowa, her mother-in-law, of most of her chores as was expected. Even though Rattowa constantly nagged about her poor cooking and perceived procrastination, she did her best and never responded verbally. She knew that this was the norm in patrilocal situations. Paradoxically, over time the nagging was gradually displaced by praise, especially when they had visitors, even though Sumintra did things no differently. This was perhaps because Rottawa came to appreciate Sumintra's worth as a domestic worker on days when Sumintra went to help in the fields and she, Rattowa, had to revert to full time domestic work.

Whenever there was no pressing work to be done in the field, Mattai would stay at home and do lighter jobs fixing things around. His lower back had started to pain and he constantly had to rest. Moreover, he kept forgetting things and sometimes looked around for his hammer, even as he was holding it, blaming others for removing his stuff. Sook, however, would do all the hard work as Mattai had done years before.

As Mattai was fixing his barbwire fence one day a stooping stranger, dressed in old clothes and carrying a half-filled, cloth shoulder bag and bracing on a crude walking stick came to his gate. It was a beggar seeking alms. Even though several beggars had already passed by that week, Rattowa told Sumintra to give him a cup of rice which he accepted, opening his shoulder sack as it was poured in. He then clasped his hands as if in prayer and muttered something inaudible. Raising his voice he then said,

"*Pani*, please," and they give him a cup of water.

As Mattai looked closer at him he thought he was familiar but could not recollect where he had seen him before. He had a long scar on the left side his face.

"Wha' yu name?" he queried.

"Garibay."

Mattai noticed that his teeth were missing. His looks, voice and name did ring a bell but Mattai could not place him and did not ask any more questions. He kept thinking of it all day but could not recall, since he was now senile, where their paths had crossed before. Was he the man who was supposed to go back to Calcutta? What was his name? Garibay. If so, did he see Mattai's parents and delivered his message? It was too late to satisfy his curiosity.

Late that night, as he pondered again, it came back to him. It was the same Garibay who

98

had borrowed money from him on the ship many years before, his *jihaji*—shipmate. How much was it? Two rupees. No, five rupees. For tobacco. He had never seen him again and had never been repaid. Divine retribution—Karma, he thought, and kept it to himself.

****

As life got better for them, Sook drank more frequently. Mattai who had gradually become demented could no longer advise him or object to his ways. He had acquired a circle of friends who helped each other in their fields. On pressing days, when there was important work to be done he would rise before dawn at the faint sounds of early morning *gana* [4] coming from the only radio in the neighborhood. He and his friends rendered "day hand" [5] by taking turns in assisting each other mainly to harvest and "shy" [6] rice. It made the work easier and saved money because it was a voluntary exchange of labor within the group. No wages

Using 'beeta' on clothes

---

[4] gana- Hindi songs, mostly from movies.
[5] day hand- helping each other/ lend a hand
[6] shy- scattering seeds manually/broadcasting seeds.

were paid. It also afforded them more leisure time. On slack days, they would graze their herds, play cards, catch fishes with their cast nets or drink.

One day they sat under a huge mango tree at Bamboo Dam playing cards and drinking the lethal combination of *Bush Rum* [7] and trench water while, at the same time, keeping an eye on their cattle grazing not far away. *Bush Rum* was illegal, cheap and readily available as it was distilled in the woodlands not far away. From their position, sitting in a circle, they could see clearly in all directions and were careful to look periodically in order to see who was coming their way. In the distance they saw some women washing clothes by the side of the canal, their *beeta* [8] rising and falling on the wet clothes as the constant echoes reached them seconds later.

"Romie," Prem said as he declared his hand of four consecutive spades, a King, Queen and Jack of Hearts. Pota then began shuffling the pack for the next game.

"Chairs," said Bantun as he lifted his dented tin cup to drink, then froze in suspended animation.

" Run," he said.

"Fuh wha'?"

"Police ah come."

His friends turned in unison and saw a lone policeman some distance away walking hurriedly towards them. Instinctively, without picking up their cards and cigarettes they all dashed towards

---

[7] Bush Rum- moonshine/illegally made rum
[8] beeta- piece of board, shaped like a Ping-Pong bat,
    used for thumping clothes.

the bushes about two hundred yards away beyond the rice fields. Cecil, who earlier was complaining about an upset stomach from a hangover and was lying on an empty rice bag nearby, outdistanced all of them by about twenty yards. Propelled by the mixture of adrenaline and alcohol, Bantun was quick to climb a huge tamarind tree and conceal himself among the dense leaves.

"Nah run. Pota!" the police shouted, "Prem!"

In their rush, they could not make out his words as they accelerated and took cover amidst the trees.

Out of breath, from their concealed position, they peered out to see if the policeman was pursuing them. To their relief and surprise he was not. Instead, he sat down leisurely under the mango tree, picked up a cup, poured himself a drink and gulped it down not even bothering

Cigarettes

to dilute it with water which was within his hand's reach. Then he lit one of their abandoned Broadway cigarettes.

He continued to drink, looking towards the bushes from time to time. The concealed men would pull back their heads whenever he looked in their direction as if it were a game of hide and seek. None of them wanted to be recognized. He was speedily taking his third drink when Bantun, from his vantage point in the tamarind tree, declared,

"Is constable Baldeo."

"Baldeo?" they repeated simultaneously.

It was only then that they realized that the policeman was Baldeo who had gradually become an al-
coholic over the years. He was always broke. He
would not arrest anyone for drinking illegal alcohol,
especially when he was offered it free. In fact, he
had not arrested anyone for anything at all for three
consecutive years, equating poor policing with good
policing.

As they emerged from their hiding places,
Baldeo greeted them, "Ah wha' yu all 'fraid of? Is
jus' a drink ah want."
They felt foolish, laughed at their own haste, happy
that it turned out that way. They took their former
positions and continued their session as Baldeo
picked up the cards and started to shuffle, making
sure he was in the game.

Convoy of Carts

11

A 'Good' Movie

While Sook spent the days around his friends and at his field and grazing his cattle, he was always at home by nightfall. He was a responsible husband. In time he fathered three children, Pinny, Ram and Mohani who was so pretty that everyone called her Dolly. He was also a dependable father. At nights he and Sumintra would sit, chat and fantasize openly of a better future, a bigger house, and family planning.

Once in a blue moon they would go to see a movie at Atlantis cinema in Suddie. This was always precipitated by the news that a "very good picture" was showing. One day they heard from a door-to-door cloth salesman that "Dosti" was show-ing. "Very good picture," he said, "Really nice." When questioned for details, he confessed that he had not seen the movie but had heard it was good, displaying one of his salesmanship qualities of praising untested products.

Sumintra, who had not seen a movie since the previous year, encouraged Sook to take her. He was persuaded even though it was the harvest sea-son with pressing, full-time work to be done. Since going to the movies was usually a grand occasion, they planned to go three days later.

On the day of the movie they stopped work-ing at one o' clock, went home, bathe and got dressed. Then, as Sook harnessed his donkey to the cart, Sumintra packed their bas-ket of food which she had prepared the night before, and drinks. They left about three and proceeded along the earthen road, going north

Rumaals / Headkerchiefs

and then east towards Suddie. As they passed Bush Lot, Reliance and Mainstay, Pota, Cecil and Coosa joined them as planned with their wives , wearing long dresses and *rumaals* [9], seated in their donkey carts.

---

[9] rumaals- also called headkerchiefs

As the convoy of carts proceeded down the burnt brick, pothole-filled road, they saw other groups heading in the same direction. Sook, who was in the lead, poked his donkey with a stick as a way of accelerating. People hailed them as they went and they exchanged greetings, adding that 'a very nice picture' was showing. As they passed Golden Fleece and Zorg, he kept looking for Guptie and "Zaag Daam," two men he knew by their reputation for being excellent cricketers. He looked on both sides of the road but could not remember where they lived.

It was getting dark when they reached Suddie. The twelve miles had taken them four hours. They tied their donkeys securely to short poles, which they referred to as 'coota'. Sook was always extra careful about this, as he did not want to have any reason to attend court. They were also careful to leave their donkeys and carts far from the cinema as they had heard of someone being turned out, with his donkey and cart, of a newly-built drive-in cinema for cars on the east coast of Demerara. The person had vehemently protested, wanting to know whether it was a drive-in or drive-out cinema.

They paid five cents each and sat on the long wooden benches in the cinema close to the large screen, the women keeping their baskets near them. The movie "Dosti " was tragically entertaining. The men with their heads strained from looking up fought back tears while the women sobbed and cried openly, wiping their tears with handkerchiefs, when they saw the suffering of a crippled boy. They did not even bother to take pleasure in the food they had dedicated so much time preparing. No one said a word so engrossed they were with the happenings on screen. No one left for the toilet or got out of their seat even though the cinema was packed. Later, as the hero's fortune changed, their spirits lifted but still no one uttered a word, not knowing what to expect next. It appeared as if what they were not looking at a movie but were experiencing actuality.

On the way back, however, once the stillness was broken they chattered incessantly as if to make up for the long silence in the cinema, and ate their food belatedly.

"Mi really sarry fuh tha' bie," Coosa said, referring to the injured hero of the film.

"Look how easy eh life change," Sook agreed, then after a short silence, added, " Was eh fate, karma."

No one seemed to realize or mention that it was acting, not even based on a true story. To discuss that would have diminished the quality of their trip and made it less worthwhile, defeated its purpose, made their tears worthless and their overall reaction foolish.

As they passed Abram Zuil and approached Hoffvonarich, popularly known as Three Bridge, everyone fell silent. Numerous stories that the place was haunted had circulated. There were claims of travelers seeing unending lines of pigs crossing the road pre-

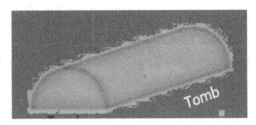

venting people from passing, especially around midnight. Other tales were of 'Dutchman' galloping on horseback carrying swords. No one disputed these accounts. Yet, nobody had met a person who actually saw these goings-on. Everything was hearsay. Still, they seemed believable because everybody had heard that the Dutch had colonized the country before the British took over. Some places like Abram Zuil and Zorg Envlygt still had Dutch names. Legend had it that some Dutchmen had committed individual or mass suicide rather than succumb to British rule. They had even entombed themselves, family members and jewelry in large cement graves. One cylindrical tomb was at the roadside in Columbia village as evidence of their unfortunate demise. Their premature deaths caused them to roam and haunt the place perpetually registering their dissatisfaction of the injustices they had suffered.

The wind coming from over the Atlantic Ocean howled as it passed through the mixed forest on the windward side of the road. As a result, the lighted *bamchodies* [10] were repeatedly blown out. No one complained; they wordlessly relighted them. Even Coosa, who usually prattled, kept absolutely quiet not wanting to attract attention to himself by being singled out by any over-zealous ghost.

"Look," whispered Pota.
"Sshhh…."

---

[10] bamchodies- flambeau, bottle lamp

A 'Good' Movie

They kept quiet as they passed a large object by the roadside. By the light of one *bamchodie* they saw what seemed to be a cow sitting by the roadside, motionless. They did not know what to make of it. As they continued they passed another large immobile object. Some of them were convinced that it was the same cow that they had passed earlier reappearing once again.

They approached Queenstown, which was named in honor of Queen Victoria of England who everyone credited for setting the slaves free. It was the most populated area for miles, inhabited by the descendants of African slaves. It was not until they entered the village and saw a few lights that they started talking again still careful not to talk about the cow, nervous that it may be a ghost accompanying them stealthily. They became silent again as they passed within a few feet of the large tomb at the roadside in Columbia.

Closer to home and back in their comfort zone, everyone, except, Sook, became talkative once again, with Coosa constantly interrupting others in order to make his point. Sook was more concerned with the progressive slothfulness of the donkey and the urgency to reach home. This led him to poke the donkey more frequently and swearing. This act of cruelty had not originated at the start of the homeward trip. In fact, the donkey seemed very enthused then and took off very energetically as any prized draught animal. However, as the miles rolled by its demeanor changed from willingness, to resigned cooperation, to ambivalence, to reluctance, to stubbornness and, finally, refusal to budge. In the same manner, Sook's countenance correspondingly shifted throughout the entire continuum: from initial high-spirited eagerness, to satisfaction, to indifference, to concern, to agitation, to vexation and eventually anger. This led him to match the donkey's decline in performance, its diminishing returns, with corrective damage control reaction, with the stubborn donkey bearing the brunt of his aggressiveness. In an effort to keep up the pace he prodded the ass with his stick and profusely rebuked it as a "lazy, good-for-nothing *gaddaha*". At the same time, none of his companions had the presence of mind or dared to suggest that they stop and take a rest. Collectively, they were afraid of ghosts and Sook who, under stressful conditions would spare no effort in redirecting his anger at them.

By three in the morning they reached home, exhausted. The next morning they were up early getting ready to harvest the rice paddies.

Dutch built church in Leguan

Kyk-Over-Al
Essequibo River

Relics of Dutch presence in Guyana

Dr. Jagan

12

The 'Savior'- Cheddi Jagan

A large group had assembled at Settlement Bridge, the large wooden bridge spanning the irrigation canal and connecting the eastern and western sections of Bush Lot settlement. They had earlier abandoned their chores, washed, dressed and converged there eagerly awaiting the arrival of Cheddi Jagan, a native member of the Legislative Assembly of British Guiana. He was to be there at two o' clock. It was already three and there was no sign of him as they patiently waited in trepidation.

Jagan was a symbol of hope for them. He had returned with Janet his American wife, whom he had met while studying dentistry in Chicago, USA, to champion the cause of the poor workers. He was the counterpart of George Price of Belize, Eric Williams of Trinidad and Tobago and Manley of Jamaica. He had traveled throughout the colony speaking to groups of people and listening to their concerns. His commitment was strengthened in 1948 when four sugar workers had been massacred by colonial police at Enmore on the East Coast of Demerara, making them martyrs. On that day he vowed to strive with all his efforts to put an end to the injustices under colonialism and improve the circumstances of the working people of British Guiana.

So the people waited, the crowd getting larger as late comers, including Sook, trickled in. Around three fifteen Paraka, who had been drinking since mid-morning, said,

"Ah tell yu all he nah guh come," as if he was privy to inside information not available to others.

"All yu' haad aaze, na like fu…."

"Shut yu ass !" Talesh respond angrily as other people turned their irritated attention to Paraka who silently retreated to the periphery of the crowd. Nevertheless, shortly afterwards people began gravitating towards others of their proclivities, disintegrating the crowd into smaller groups. Some of the men sat on the edge of the bridge with their feet dangling as they tapped cigarette ashes in the water below. Others stood in small circles on the road expounding issues as if Jagan was already with them.

"Without wata wi can't plant de next rice crap," Lay Lay wailed.

"De price fu rice so low, wi can haadly feed wi family," Beharry complained.

" É comin'."

111

All conversation stopped and heads turned together to the east. A lone car was approaching with a cloud of dust, due to the long dry season, in its trail.

People stepped to the roadsides as it approached and came to a standstill. It was a black Morris Oxford car. The driver emerged, followed by three other men, each opening the door for himself. The crowd gathered around the car uncertain as to who was Dr. Jagan until a lady passed through and placed a *mala* [1] around his neck. Then everyone realized that the tall, handsome, energetic-looking, young man was the leader, Dr. Cheddi Jagan. They had expected him to be much older. Only then did they step backwards and gave him some space as he clasped his hands as if in prayer, said "Thank you" and walked forward. Ramphal, a village leader ushered him to a table with four chairs in the middle of the bridge, the platform for the meeting.

"Good afternoon, brothers and sisters," Dr. Jagan said without sitting down.

"I am happy to come and visit with you."

There was complete silence as some impressed people thought that he had traveled all the way from America. In fact, he had just come from Richmond, a village not far away. He was on a countrywide tour which had started three weeks before in his village of Port Mourant in Berbice.

"I know you all have a lot of problems and I will do my best to help you," he said without preliminaries.

---

[1] mala-garland

"I will see to it that this bumpy road is paved, this trench is clean and that you all get regular water supply for your rice."

The people paid rapt attention. Those were some of the exact things they wanted.

"I will build a school for your children."

They were enthused.

"And provide a medical clinic, with a full-time doctor."

They were pleased.

"I will raise the price of rice. The capitalists and imperialists are plundering our wealth."

They were thrilled as they stood in awe, wanting to hear more.

"I will see to it that you get electricity in every house."

They were electrified. This was the ultimate. It was more than they were going to ask for. Dr. Jagan was truly God-sent. Even as he paused to drink some coconut water that they offered him no one asked any question or made any comment. Everyone eagerly awaited his next words.

"The French peasants revolted and overthrew the imperialist king in the middle of the last century. The Russian people overthrew the imperialist Tzar in 1917 and set up a communist state where there are no rich and poor. [2] No one is starving. In Russia, everyone get free education and medical treatment. No one suffers, no one is unemployed, no one rob or thief from others. That is what we want here, my brothers and sisters. What we

---

[2] He was referring to the French and Russian revolutions.

want is a socialist state. Scientific Socialism is the solution to all our problems."

Dr. Jagan paused for effect. He wanted the people to marinate in and digest what he was saying. Paraka, thinking that his speech was over, got up from the grassy slope he was sitting on and clapped. The crowd followed impulsively with a loud applause that reverberated in the nearby woodlands. After a minute, Dr. Jagan raised his hand charismatically and they fell silent.

"We don't need capitalists like America and England to take away our riches. You know what they do? They buy our raw materials— our rice, our sugar, our bauxite, our lumber— for a pittance and sell us their products for an exorbitant price. They are the ones who cause us to suffer so much. I will find different markets for our products, markets in Russia, Cuba, Poland and other communist bloc countries. Then the price of rice will raise and you all will be better off.

"Capitalism is moribund. It is failing everywhere. What we need is dictatorship by the proletariat. The people have to take charge; they have to run their affairs. We will set up cells, which will govern each village, every community, and report to the central committee of the party. The people will tell us what they need and we will provide for them."

He took another sip. The people did not understand most of what he had just said but they applauded energetically. They were contented. Sook's value for education was rekindled as he participated.

"What we need now is independence," he continued.

"We do not need the British to govern us. We have enough educated people to head our police force, defense force and public service; to form our own government. We don't need foreigners to boss us. You all need to get registered and vote in the next elections so that your children can have a better life."

More thunderous applause. They wanted a savior and here was one in flesh and blood, one of their own; one whose forefathers, like theirs, had worked on the sugar plantations.

In the end there were no questions as Dr. Jagan had promised all they needed, and more. He and his small entourage were escorted by Ramphal for dinner as the crowd dispersed, some following at a remote distance while a few men were left sitting on the bridge dangling their feet.

"We need a school fu we children," Paraka requested to no one in particular. No one paid him any mind as they walked away.

Burnham and Jagan

Several years later, Dr. Jagan, then Premier, was imprisoned as the British declared a state of emergency. This happened after the main opposition political party organized widespread demon-

John F. Kennedy and Dr. Jagan
Washington D.C; 1962

strations and the American CIA financed prolong strikes and riots which manifested itself by extensive arson, plundering, killing and rape. Many of Dr. Jagan's followers were victims as the country was divided racially among Indo-Guyanese and Afro-Guyanese.

This destabilization was because the cold war was in effect and they were afraid that British Guiana under Jagan would become a communist state. [3] Top American officials strongly felt that, "an independent British Guiana under Burnham (Jagan's opponent) ...would cause us many fewer problems than an independent Guiana under Jagan." [4] Thus, their need to oust him.

Years afterwards communism failed and collapsed. It became known that the communist system in Russia and other places was fraught with hypocrisy, double standards, empty promises and dictatorship by a few people and not the majority. The rich leaders and their families, the bourgeois, were living in luxury while many of the poor masses, the proletariat, were bullied, starved, tortured, imprisoned, overworked and killed. On the other hand, only the party faithfuls, lackeys, stooges and 'wannabees' were saved from this miserable existence as they enjoyed privileged lives. Communism, even Scientific Socialism, was good on paper, in theory; not in practice. More countries turned to capitalism

---

[3] American President John F. Kennedy himself, after a meeting with Dr. Jagan in 1962, expressed doubts as to whether Dr. Jagan would be able to sustain his position as a parliamentary democrat. "I have a feeling," he said, "that in a couple of years he will find ways to suspend his constitutional provisions and will cut his opposition off at the knees... Parliamentary democracy is going to be damn difficult in a country at this stage of development... it's going to be almost impossible for Jagan to concentrate the energies of his country on development through a parliamentary system"
A THOUSAND DAYS John F. Kennedy In The White House by Arthur M. Schlesinger, Jr. (1965) p. 777
[4] *Ibid*, p. 779

which emerged as the better political and economic system.

After 28 years as Leader of the Opposition, Dr. Jagan, more aged and mellow and with the advantage of experience and hindsight, was elected as the President of Guyana in 1992. This was facilitated through fair and free elections observed by members of the Carter Center, of the USA, and other international observers.

President Jagan

****

For decades later parents related to their children of the time when Dr. Jagan had visited, of the meeting at Settlement Bridge and the things he had promised. They would lament over the idea that they would have long enjoyed these things if the Americans and the British colonial rulers had not forced him out of public office.

13

Mattai's Reincarnation

"Dahin!" Sook hollered as the stood on the long slippery rake pulled by his yoked oxen. The pair of bulls turned obediently as if they were in training, obeying the command of a drill sergeant. Actually, they were accustomed to this exercise which they did twice a year. Sook, his toes bent for stability, was preparing his rice field for the next crop. He traversed the flooded field in this manner leveling it as well as clearing it of weeds. As he moved, large long-necked flocks of white 'cranes' flapped their wings and reluctantly took off avoiding the approaching oxen. They alighted elsewhere and continued their search for worms and other small, edible animals, only to repeat this maneuver minutes later as the oxen advanced towards them again.

Every now and then he would shout "Hoa!" and the trained oxen would stop. He would step off the rake into the mud, bend and pass his fingers between the spiked teeth in order to remove accumulated grass and compost.

For the most part the sky was clear with a few cirrostratus clouds in the northeast, reminding Sook of the impression left by waves on the beach. As he looked around he could see other farmers working in their fields, some of them accompanied by their family members who did different tasks. Quite a few were also raking while others were chopping with cutlasses, digging with shovels or pulling intruding weeds with their bare hands, a task reserved for children. In the distance some women were in the shallow, muddy drainage canal fishing with their round hand seines while their small, half-naked children were playing in the water and on the adjacent earthen dams.

Bigger boys, unsupervised, were bathing in the deeper irrigation canal on the other side of the fields. Sook could hear their calls, shouts and yells as they ran, plunged and dived. The center of attraction was a few of them who were floating on a crude raft made of buoyant tree trunks lashed together with vines. They kept it moving to and fro with a bamboo pole. Younger boys who could not swim followed on the escarpment pleading eagerly for a ride. Many of them had neglected their chores of watching their cattle graze in areas predetermined by their fathers. They hoped that their activities would never be discovered. This only happened occasionally when the cattle strayed and ate the rice plants nearby. Then, the enraged father would invariably vent his anger and disappointment by whipping his son soundly with his leather belt or a whip broken from a nearby tree, preferably a tamarind tree, cursing and chasing the boy if he was elusive. Thereafter, the punished child would become more responsible in doing his assigned chore for a while before gradually relapsing. Then the entire scenario will be repeated, creating a cycle.

Sook did not allow Sumintra to go catching fish as he thought it was below their newly achieved status. Their field had yielded bountifully for several years and they had opened a savings account in a bank, an act that was guarded as top secret. They had even bought a bicycle and an iron-framed bed.

Across several fields he could see Lashup's son, Showkat, chopping away tirelessly. Lashup rarely went to the 'Back Dam' always complaining that his foot, which he had accidentally chopped several years before, was aching. Some people thought that he was feigning sickness due to laziness. This popular feeling was sub-

Trundling 'wheela'

stantiated by the fact that he was not plaintive when walking around drinking and socializing, which he did almost daily.

Presently, Sook noticed a small boy approaching trundling a *wheela* [1] by hitting it consistently with a stick and jogging behind. As he came closer Sook recognized him as his neighbor's son, Budso.

"Hoa ! Wha' happen, bie?" he asked as Budzo came within earshot.

"A'ntie say yu mus' come quick," Budzo said breathing heavily. Sook assumed he was talking about Sumintra. In the settlement, women were referred to as 'auntie', 'nani' or 'agie' by children according to their age and relationship, titles which became honorary and a show of respect when people were unrelated.

"Fuh wha'?" Sook inquired.

No one ever sent for him while he was working mainly because his field was far from his house. Also, his family knew too well how seriously he took farming and would not call him away for what he considered to be petty reasons, even when they thought it was crucial. His gut feeling was that something had seriously gone wrong.

"She seh must hurry an' come quick," Budzo continued as if he had not heard Sook's question.

Sook dropped the reins, stepped off the rake and headed for home at a vigorous pace. He did not run even though he had an intuition that something was terribly wrong.

"Tie them bull fu mi," he instructed Budzo as he went.

---

[1] wheela- old, discarded bicycle wheel or tire that
   children rolled.

Taking a short cut, cross-country route, Sook approached his home within twenty-five minutes. From a distance he noticed a small group of people in his yard. He recognized Sadoo, who was obese, from afar with his oiled, baldpate reflecting the mid-afternoon sun. Isahak and Polo, among others, were also noticeable in the gathering. As he entered the yard he asked,

"Wha' happen?"

"Yu father black out," Jadoo said.

He rushed into house, took one look at Mattai lying on a cot and realized that it was very serious. A woman was pressing 'smelling salts', wrapped in a handkerchief, on his nose while others looked on. He did not stir.

"Gina gaan fuh call dacta Ali," Sumintra told him, sobbing. Sook did not know what to do. Head bent, he stepped back outside among the men. There was a moment of silence when no one thought of anything appropriate to say. It ended when Sadoo said,

"Mattai wuk too haad fuh his old age," as if performing an autopsy. Sadoo who looked as if he had never missed a meal was, as usual, neatly dressed complete with shoes. He himself hardly did any work, preferring to let his two grown sons support the family while he walked around the village, flirting and womanizing as if he had been mandated to do so by the Governor in a concerted effort to keep the population from decreasing. He did not touch alcohol believing that his way of life was superior to any hardworking man who drank. He had witnessed such men beating their wives. Abstaining, he thought, would absolve him from his immoral acts

123

and wrongdoings. It was rumored that he had fathered seven children out of wedlock by five different women. He would always smile charmingly when asked about this, never confirming or denying the allegation.

"Eh res' too much," Isahak contradicted as if he had not heard what Sadoo said just a few seconds before.

"Need fuh exacise."

Rattowa said that he did not take his tablets for hypertension but drank bush medicine instead. Sook sat and bowed his head helplessly, distressed. He knew that what some of the people were saying was not exactly true but was in no mood to set things straight.

After several hours doctor Ali arrived in his large brown car. He examined Mattai briefly, checking his pulse, eyes, and mouth and pronounced him dead.

He women, lead by Rattowa, started wailing in harmony. The men backed off and stood under the large 'Long Mango' tree in the yard.

"Mattai bin ah whan rale good man," Polo eulogized.

"Rale good," Blue echoed.

"Never gat ahn enemy all eh life," Isahak extolled.

No one disputed them as each focused on good things Mattai had done.

14

The Funeral

The communal spirit of the people of Bush Lot settlement, especially in times of need, helped Sook and his family manage their tragedy and made it more bearable. A tent was rapidly attached to the house by the men while the women cooked and prepared tea and coffee for the first night of wake. People came from near and far in waves. As if by arrangement neighbors came first, then people from neighboring villages. By nightfall people were arriving from as far as Devonshire Castle, six miles away, the village where Sumintra originated.

The Funeral

The women, heads covered with *orhnis* [2], crowded into the house some crying and consoling Rattowa and Sumintra, some busy cooking and preparing tea and coffee. The older men sat outside on benches borrowed from the primary school. They chatted about religion, politics and farming. Their common concern was the foreseeable water shortage. Their field needed to be flooded for the seeds to be broadcasted, to 'shy rice' as they called it. Every now and then one of them would gave a one line tribute to Mattai as if to reconcile some wrong he had done to Mattai in the past and had not apologized for while the opportunity existed. It was as if Mattai was listening, hearing confessions. Suddenly, their conversation was interrupted by,

"Time fuh guh now!"

All activity stopped temporarily as they turned and saw Gadar's wife. Without waiting to hear the end of the episode Coosa was describing, Gadar, who was now in his eighties, left wordlessly.

Cremating Mattai

Some of them gave silent credibility to Coosa who

[2] orhni-thin scarves

had on numerous occasions said that Gadar's wife was ruling him. They shook their heads, turned around and paid even more attention to him as he continued.

The young men sat in circles on empty rice bags spread on the ground, playing cards. The players were surrounded by onlookers eager to replace those who lost and were " knocked out". Meanwhile, at the back of the house Sunalall, a local carpenter, made a coffin with the assistance of his son. It was his way of 'pitching in' as he usually did.

Sook mingled with the crowd, solemnly shaking hands, accepting condolences, and distributing cigarettes. Pinny, Ram and Dolly, along with women relatives assisted in serving tea, coffee and biscuits and cooked meals to the crowd.

Two days later Mattai was cremated at Reliance foreshore. A huge crowd converged there to pay their last respects. Sook, who was the only son, took part in the ceremony lead by pundit Chowbay near the funeral pyre. Prayers were said as a small procession walked ceremoniously around the pyre several times then lighted it. The fire, fueled by ghee, soon enlarged and engulfed the pyre, causing the crowd to retreat gradually from the intense heat. They moved backwards almost unanimously, one step at a time, enlarging the circumference of the already large circle. From a distance they stood watching.

After a while people started to depart. Friends and family members stayed behind until the wood, coffin and body of Mattai had turned to ashes three hours later. All the while, Rattowa, Sumintra and Rambasie, who had arrived from Philadelphia the previous night, wailed and sobbed alternately.

The following morning the family of Mattai returned, scooped up the ashes into metal containers, walked into the waters of the nearby Atlantic Ocean and scattered it dutifully. It was what Mattai had wanted, to allow his soul to be set free and transmigrate as soon as possible after he died. It was part of the never-ending process of reincarnation.

The wake continued for nine nights with the crowd diminishing with each passing night, until only relatives and neighbors remained.

15

A Taste of Success

Sook's family increased with the birth of Latch, Doodie, Chines and Jaggie. With no family planning or birth control children were born within a few years of each other, sometimes less. The children were all raised with 'tough love', a mixture of strict discipline and parental affection, the equivalent of benevolent dictatorship. Sook made it a point to send them all to school even though it meant harder work for him. It was his duty. His own experience had caused him to struggle to read and write, the only two things which he did very slowly and only when absolutely necessary. Whenever he thought of this he remembered the encounter with Mr. Wint and his father. He, not infrequently, wondered what would have happened if he had gone to school further? What job would he be doing? Maybe he would have become a clerk in the office or even a judge. Would he have married Sumintra? Many years before, he had become aware that one of his former classmates, Rahaman, had gone to England and became a lawyer. In fact, Rahaman had come looking for him dressed in his black suit, tie and felt hat. Regrettably, he had been working in his rice field and no one sent for him because Rahaman was busy with only a few minutes to spare and a taxicab waiting for him.　　Consequently, Sook valued education and wanted his children to be educated. He told them that he wanted them to become doctors and lawyers. Whenever he came home after a hard day's work and found them playing, which he considered idling, he would yell commandingly,"Guh tek yu book ahn read!" angrily. After a time the first to see him coming would shout "Daddy ah come!" and they would cease playing and retreat to their rooms or revert to their incomplete chores. It reminded Chines of the story "Belling the Cat" which he had read in his standard two reading book.The children did not realize that Sook cared about their future. They thought that he was being mean. In reality, he was more of a considerate master who thought that he was working hard and the least his children could do was to study hard in return for the privilege of going to school. He would reinforce this regularly by mentioning that many other neighboring children were taken out of school early to work. Nevertheless, when school was out the boys, especially Latch and Doodie, would have to go daily to work in the rice field and vegetable plot adjacent to it. They detested this since they knew that boys with less stringent fathers allowed them to go play cricket, swim and idle. They, on the other hand, were constantly pulling 'nut grass', watering, mulching and tilling the soil. On long beds, they cultivated okras, peppers,

po/ posie/ bedpan/chamber pot

balangay [3], *poi* [4], as well as other leaf crops and legumes, especially *bora* [5]. They also tended *carila* [6] and squash, called 'lowka' by Sook, which hung like huge Christmas decorations on a *machan* [7]. Nearby, they also had clumps of banana trees which they always harvested before they were ripe, always mindful of the prying eyes of thieves who committed praedial larceny as a matter of course. One man in particular, a very dark Indian known as Black Bud looked suspicious, always inspecting the crops, staring pass the used, weather beaten *poe* [8] mounted on a post to ward off *bad-eye*. [9] He passed regularly straining under giant bunches of bananas or plantains unsteadily perched on his head. His two hands were always occupied holding bags of vegetables and his sharp cutlass. No one knew where his farm

---

[3] balangay-eggplant
[4] poi- spinage
[5] bora-string beans/long beans
[6] carila- bitter melon/cerosie/kerele
[7] machan-large table-like structure to support spreading plants
[8] poe-chamber pot
[9] bad-eye- the evil eye, which according to superstition is a bad omen.

was. They suspected him of stealing daily but could not prove it, being afraid to follow or question him.

This continued every Easter, summer and Christmas break. The boys were only excused when it rained heavy and continuously, not light and intermittently. Chines went occasionally and Jaggie, who was younger, was allowed to stay home with his sisters who did all the household work. It was not until many years later that some of them realized that Sook's interest in their education outweighed the hard work he had them doing. Only in retrospect did they realize that other boys were working as hard year round without getting the opportunity to attend school, an advantage which they had but did not particularly want at the time.

****

Years later, Sook moved once again building a big wooden four-bedroom house two miles away in Anna Regina. He was moving with the flow as others at Bush Lot settlement were also resettling. Their new location was near a big canal which everyone called a
'big trench', not far from the Atlantic Ocean to the north and the huge rice factory to the south. Other

Radio..with buttons

children— Data and Sandra—were added to the family. The children liked this new location. The 'high house' was built on sturdy cement pillars, making it possible for

132

the children to play underneath, something they could not do at their former ranch style-house. In addition, it was painted white with a red roof and furnished with a sofa, 'couch' and wardrobe with a long mirror. When Sook received a lump-sum payment for his paddy sold at the factory, he added a huge Grundig radio with a heavy, external Pertrix battery.

It fascinated everyone including the adults who curiously pressed the keys, which they called buttons. Initially, they were more concerned with the functions than the programs. It was meticulously guarded and the children were prevented from touching it least it malfunctioned or stopped working altogether. In time, the entire setting was enhanced by bright lights from two forty-watt bulbs and a fluorescent lamp made possible by a drive to electrify the area.

External Radio Battery

As the boys grew older, they spent endless hours in the canal swimming and playing water sports in their spare time, coming home with red eyes only at mealtime. Such luxury, however, was contingent on the amount of work to be done at the 'back dam', the name for rice field and farm located in the backlands. However, to their advantage, their new location was closer to the schools around. No longer did they have to walk two miles daily to school. Since many of their former neighbors from Bush Lot settlement now lived further away, they made new friends and got new neighbors.

A Taste of Success

In time, Doodie migrated to Canada estranging himself from the family and discouraging them from joining him by saying, in one of his few letters, that Canada was "not a bed of roses". Latch went on to become a teacher, then a successful lawyer studying at the University of the West Indies. Thereafter, he moved to Belize (formerly British Honduras) where he became known as Lutch (short for Lutchman Sooknandan). He progressed, becoming the Director of Public Prosecutions having been promoted from Crown Counsel, the equivalent of State Prosecutor. Chines went to the University of Guyana and also left to teach in Belize where he became known as (Karan) Chand. The girls married and moved on. As Sook made more material progress he opened a rum shop, called a 'club' by many even though it was a public bar with no membership requirements. He achieved this partially by making cement blocks, single-handedly, a small batch at a time after work. Then he enlisted the help of construction workers to do the building. His youngest son Jaggie, a very talented dancer, discontinued his education and became the bartender. Business was good mainly because of the culture of drinking in rural farming communities and, to some extent, the custom of serving drinks on credit.

Sook gradually eased himself from farming and stayed home, proud of his investment. His increased leisure time was facilitated by mechanization in the rice industry which made it less labor intensive. Tractors would plow the fields and huge reapers, called combines, would harvest and thresh the rice paddies. By this time, he had passed middle age and little by little was going into retirement. He and Sumintra would sit and talk about bygone days, proud of their progress, yet sometimes cheerless that their house was almost an empty nest.[10]

Jaggie, Pinnie, RP, Sook,Karan, Jenny, Data, Dolly

---

[10] The "Empty Nest Syndrome" is a term used by psychologists, sociologists and other social scientists for the circmstance when children grow up and leave their parents' home (almost empty) to live on their own.

16

"O. Land of the Free…"

The Boeing 747 Taca airplane cruised thirteen thousand feet above the Caribbean Sea heading southwest from Miami. After nearly three hours it started to descend and window seat passengers who gazed out saw the cayes—large and small—linked by broad lines of white foam where the large waves crashed on the even larger barrier reef, the second largest in the world. From above, it looked like a gigantic clothesline in a storm. Further west, the sea continuously rinsed the jagged Belizean coastline as if cleansing it of the ubiquitous garbage and other pollutants deposited by the many rivers. Adjacent to it, the coastal plain, dominated in some areas by

136

numerous trees and marshlands, was dotted with dwelling houses and other buildings.

After a short while the plane circled the Philip Goldson International Airport.[1] Alert passengers saw a small building similar to a dwelling house. It was actually the terminal building,[2] with people on top, some sitting with their feet hanging over the sides. Their undivided attention followed the plane as it touched down, hitting the tarmac with a bump, and taxied to a stop after making a one hundred and eighty degrees turn.

After clearing immigration and customs Chand boarded Stanley's taxi, a very large spacious brown Ford car, to Belize City.

"Where yu fram?" Stanley, a friendly looking Garifuna, wanted to know as he sped east into Ladyville.

"Guyana."

They turned right unto the main road proceeded south towards Belize City.

"Guyana, Guyana, Guyana," Stanley repeated, tapping the steering wheel three times and inclining his head, trying to jog his memory. "Ghana? In Africa?"

He was amazed.

"No, no, not in Africa. In South America. Is a mainland country like Belize."

"Really?"

"Yes, is a Caribbean country just like Belize."

---

[1] Then called Belize International Airport but later named after the late Belizean patriot, lawyer and statesman, Philip S. W. Goldson.

[2] This was replaced in the 1990's by a modern airport.

In fact, Belize and Guyana are similar in many respects. Both were once British colonies— Belize in Central America and Guyana, ten times larger, in South America. Both are the only officially English-speaking countries in their region, Belize bordered by Mexico and Guatemala and Guyana by Venezuela, Brazil and Surinam. On one side of Belize there is the tranquil Caribbean Sea while the huge, boisterous Atlantic Ocean embraces Guyana.

As they passed Roses Paper Factory, the Belize Flour Mill and two lumberyards, Chand could not help realizing that Belize and Guyana have similar economies. Overtime, he became aware that the similarities are greater than he first thought. In extractive industries they grow sugar cane, rice, coconuts, citrus and have fishing and forestry. In manufacturing, they have light industries such as soft drinks, alcohol, furniture and craft while service industries include tourism, communications and banking. The difference is that Guyana mine gold, diamond and bauxite, the stuff we get aluminum from, while Belize mine a small amount of dolomite, a sedimentary rock used as fertilizer.

They crossed BelCan Bridge and saw a group of basketball players and their fans outside the Civic Center on Central American Boulevard, passed Mando's Grocery & Hardware on the right and Malik's on the left. They following vehicles and cyclists, some of whom rode recklessly staring as if daring drivers to touch them. The few pedestrians on the sidewalks, dressed casually, were going in both directions. Two young *Mestizo* [3] girls were selling tamales out of 'pig tail' buckets. Chand smiled as he recalled Mexican-American comedian George Lopez saying on TV that his mother always bought him *tamales* for Christmas just so that he could have something to unwrap.

The peoples of Belize and Guyana are also similar, comprising of descendants of African slaves, East Indian indentured servants, indigenous Indians, Caucasians and mixed, although of different proportions.

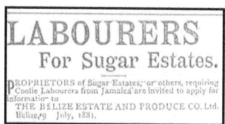

LABOURERS
For Sugar Estates.

PROPRIETORS of Sugar Estates, or others, requiring Coolie Labourers from Jamaica are invited to apply for information to
THE BELIZE ESTATE AND PRODUCE CO. Ltd.
Belize, 9 July, 1881.

Some East Indians transmigrated form Jamaica

Hence, both countries are multiracial and, thus, multicultural with diverse peoples enriching the mosaic of humanity; blending in the urban areas as 'melting pots', [4] coexisting —sometimes in enclaves— in the rural areas as 'salad bowls'. [5]

---

[3] Mesitzo-biracial mixture of Hispanic/Spaniard and native Indian.

[4] Melting Pot- when peoples of different cultures mix and mingle, adapt each other's culture, blend and acculturate creating a common culture. In the process they mutually loose aspects of their own culture and acquire others.

[5] Salad Bowl- when cultures coexist in a plural society and still maintain their peculiar features / opposite of ' Melting Pot'.

Stanley turned left unto Cemetery Lane. A large, mixed group of people was gathered at Pound Yard Bridge listening to a politician standing on a small wooden stage as he hollered over the PA system.

"And you know what? They thief we blind. The bloated contracts, the sweetheart deals for their …"

It occurred to Chand that allegations of corruption were common to both countries, also.

However, in other ways there are differences. Belize has a bicameral legislature comprising of a Senate and House of Representatives while Guyana has a unicameral legislature of only one parliamentary house. Moreover, whereas Belize has a first-past-the-post electoral system, Guyana has proportional representation. Additionally, Belize is a constitutional monarchy with a Governor General representing the Queen as Head of State whereas Guyana is a republic. However, the similarities— in history, landscape, economy, politics and culture — by far outweigh the differences between these two countries even though they are on opposite sides of the Caribbean, separated by thousands of miles.

****

It was the tenth day of September. Chand perused the Amandala newspaper as he breakfasted on fried *Jacks* [6], scrambled eggs and coffee at North Front Street Guest House. 'Belize now Belice' was the front-page feature story. The census results had just been released. It reported how the mass influx of Central American Hispanics had drastically changed the demographic composition of the country, marginalizing the 'Creoles' [7] who had formerly been the majority group. On the following page, the editorial, under the caption 'The Hispanisation of Belize', dealt at length with the same issue. As if to accelerate and accentuate the change, the Creoles were migrating north, going to the United States of America.

For decades the poor peoples of Latin America have suffered because of unfair land distribution and the capitalist policies of the rich landowners and politicians who had exploited and mislead them. They realized that the sparsely populated Belize, with its porous borders, democratic government and relative peace was the place to seek refuge and strive for a better life. And so they came in trickles and waves, legally and illegally contributing to the development of their host country and at the

---

[6] Fried Jacks- called 'fried bread' in other places and 'bakes' in Guyana.
[7] Creoles- Blacks, people of African descent sometimes mixed with European blood.

same time being resented by some for their encroachment.

People were passing in groups going to participate in or watch the parade commemorating the Battle of St. George's Caye. The battle itself, a controversial event, was supposed to have taken place in September 1798. At that time, Spain could not effectively occupy all the lands in the 'New World' which it claimed as a result of the Treaty of Tordesillas (of 1494). [8] Spaniards only sought to intervene when others settle them, attempting to drive them out as trespassers.

Some claim that there was no battle because no one was injured or died, except from diseases. Others insist that the fight was fierce and the British colonists and their slaves routed the Spaniards off shore in the vicinity of St. George's Caye which, at that time, was the capital of Belize. Whether there was bloody, physical contact or not, it is significant to note that there was some sort of close encounter which the Spaniards did not want to recur and so they did not return to threaten the settlers in the Bay of Honduras. In any case, the settlers were victorious and, thus, the need to celebrate. Two centuries later, it did not seem to matter whose ancestors had won or lost the battle; people of all races participated. As Chand walked down Albert Street he heard reggae, soca and Belizean music blasting from large, stacked 'Boom Boxes' which played so loud-

---

[8] The omnipotent Pope Alexander 1V had drawn a line, from north to south in the Atlantic Ocean, on the map of the world dividing it into two hemispheres. By a Papal Bull (decree/directive) he had awarded all newly discovered lands west of the line to Spain, and those east to Portugal.

ly as if to outdo each other. He passed people busy setting up and stocking their stalls for the anticipated sales after the parade. There was the permeating, tantalizing aroma of bar-b-qued chicken and pork, mixed with mouth-watering Creole dishes such as Rice and Beans with meat and Boil-Up and the equally salivating Hispanic food, notably Tamales, Tacos, Burritos, Enchiladas and Garnaches. Jointly they marinated the atmosphere. There were also several booths stacked with soft drinks, Belikin Beer, Caribbean Rum and other favorite drinks.

Further away, Belizeans at home, Belizean-Americans back home for the September celebrations and tourists lined both sides of Central American Boulevard awaiting for the parade to pass. Many were sheltering with umbrellas from the high temperature in the eighties. Nearby, on the balconies of houses and in some cases on the tops, people and their guests were also crowded, drinking and chatting as they eagerly waited. The music became louder as the bands approached. There were representatives from the two political parties (the PUP and UDP), followed by costume bands. The children bands were well organized even though some of the children seemed tired at this time. Their trainers kept running up and down giving them water and words of encouragement. They were followed by the big bands. Stone Jam was large and very energetic, its contingent gyrating to the music of Byron Lee and the Dragoneers.

"Cent."

The costumed members braced themselves and moved their hips to the left in unison.

"Five cents."
All hips moved to the right.
"Ten cents."
Waists moved backwards.
"Dalla."
Forward thrust.
The tempo increased
"Cent, five cent, ten cent, dalla."
Stone Jam, thoroughly rehearsed, responded accordingly with swift, sexually suggestive movements as the vocalist, after other lyrics, continued with "Gimme dalla, gimme dalla, gimme dalla, gimme dalla..."
Repeated forward thrusts, with gusto. It was well

September Carnival in Belize

choreographed and precisely executed.
The crowd roared.

The trip to see the parade had been made worthwhile. Next came 'floats', decorated trucks and other vehicles filled with revelers and loud music. One had a steel band which was playing "Oh, Land of the free by the Carib Sea", the National Anthem.

As the parade petered out some people followed it to the National Stadium [9] to witness the final performance and competition. Others converged on Albert Street to eat drink, dance and mill around until nightfall only to remove to other venues and continue the celebration.

---

[9] Later renamed "The Marion Jones Sporting Complex" after American Olympic Gold Medalist whose parents are from Belize.

Blue Hole Atoll

17

"…by the Carib Sea"

The year was 1993. Chand walked along Princess Margaret Drive, Belize City. Droves of uniformed boys on bicycles passed him on their way home, some speeding as if intent on winning a race. He too was going home from St. John's College where he taught Social Studies, History and Geography.

He felt lucky to have secured a job at such a prestigious Catholic high school even though he was not a Catholic, not even a Christian. When asked, he would tell people had he was in a state of limbo as far

Mr. Karan Chand
Teacher-St. John's College
Belize. 1996

146

as religion was concerned. This was partially because he had grown up in a Hindu family and had
not been religious because he did not understand
Hindi, the language used at religious ceremonies.
On the other hand, he did not feel comfortable in
Christian places of worship because he did not have
the background and religious knowledge. Thus, his
rationale for his intermediate state.

As he walked, he remembered how he had been
anxious at the job interview. He had probably been
tactless when he had forthrightly told the priest who
interviewed him,
" Father, I do not know if this would jeopardize my
chances of getting a job, but I am not very religious.
However, I am God fearing. I believe in being vir-
tuous, doing good things."
Father Murphy, the Jesuit priest, had looked directly
at him and replied,
" Not at tall, Karan, we have teachers of different
religions here. You don't have to be holy." In hindsight, he wondered if he should have volunteered
such personal information in a professional setting.
In Guyana, where he came from, people had been
blacklisted and victimized for less than that.

He recalled how while drinking in Guyana
he had gotten high and embarrassed an Education
Officer, a person of high rank in the Ministry of
Education.
"You are nothing but an opportunistic booth-
licker," he had said, " A government stooge."
The officer initially had only smiled and continued
to drink not wanting to be argumentative, as he had
only been invited to a drink.

"You can vote out the government at next elections," he had advised.

"Voting was only a physical exercise, not an exercise in democracy," Chand had retorted angrily reinforcing the popular feelings that elections had been rigged.

People within earshot, seated around wooden tables had laughed, some of them suppressing their snickering not wanting the officer to see them enjoying his moment of embarrassment and his lack of repartee. Not long before, the same officer had referred to them scornfully as 'Rumshop Revolutionaries, without gall'. As a result, they secretly wanted him to be insulted by someone who was educated and eloquent, qualities they themselves lacked. They were thrilled that someone was talking on their behalf, as if they all were being represented in a class action law suit. At the same time, they did not want it to appear as if they had been taking sides. Thus, they were very cautious and covert in their reactions.

In this way, the conversation had gone on ranging from friendly to indifferent to hostile, entertaining the people around who ceased all discussion of their own and passively paid rapt attention. Kat Pat sat apart from the rest, a solitary drinker. He was pathologically shy and retiring when sober. He had been there since the bar opened that morning announcing quietly how urgently he needed an 'eye-opener' [1], as if it was scarce, life-saving, pre-

---

[1] eye-opener-first drink in the morning after a night
of drinking/ opposite of nightcap

scription medication. After the first shot, his hands stopped trembling and he stayed on as usual assisting Jaggie in packing crates, relaying drinks and ice to the patrons and mopping the wet tables; always returning to his bar stool, his base of operation. In return he was remitted cigarettes, one at a time, and shots of XM Rum blended with Pepsi. Like the rest, he had followed noiselessly every word as the exchange evolved, his head moving from speaker to speaker as if watching a ping-pong game in slow motion. Emboldened by alcohol, his face contorted and without prior indication, not even clearing his throat which he usually does as a prelude to speaking, he suddenly got off the bar stool shakily. He approached the Education Officer unsteadily, wagged his finger in his face and prophesied, "People like yu guh ded bad, yu frigging *gaddaha* ! [2] I have the mind to......"

He had to be restrained by Jaggie, Sook's son and barman, a difficult task even though he, Kat Pat, was thin and fragile looking. He was escorted out resisting and cursing, not before the officer, bent on having the last word, called after him, " You blasted good-for-nothing, *rangatang*." [3]

---

[2] gaddaha-jackass
[3] rangatang-corruption of the word orangutan   /large ape

As Chand walked home from school in Belize City he did not know whether incidents like
these had caused him to be persecuted by the educa-

Swing Bridge, Belize City

tion officials some of whom one could not trust.
Generally people, especially lower level government employees distrusted them because they, like
some house slaves and plantation drivers, snitched
on others as a way of securing their privileged positions. In the end, Chand had voted with his feet by
migrating to Belize.

He crossed over the swing bridge that linked
north and south sides of Belize City, hailed Ismael
"Tony" Requena, a fellow teacher from Anglican
Cathedral College, passed Brodies superstore and
Nova Scotia Bank. The evening sun was bright and
the sidewalks were busy with school children. He
turned right into Dean Street. As he passed Dit's
Restaurant he remembered an incident that Coosa
had related in Guyana at Mattai's wake. He had ar-
ticulately related how he had gone into a restaurant
in Georgetown and inquired,
"Yu serve 'guana hay?" According to him the
waiter, an old Chinese woman, had look at him
'from head to foot' and said,

150

"We serve anybody, take a seat." Coosa had laughed heartily at his own joke while his audience, not understanding, just sat in awe, impressed by the thought of Coosa visiting the large capital city far away. Chand smiled as he recalled the night vividly as if it had happened recently. He stopped by Kick Down Fence, a popular Chinese shop, and bought snacks for his two children, Elizabeth and Romain, who attended Grace Primary School but were supposed to be home before him.

As he approached home he saw the black Pathfinder SUV of his brother, Lutch, parked infront of his home, unusual for that time in the day. His gut feeling was that something was amiss. In his apartment Sita, his wife, was seated with Lutch and

The author and family in Belize, circa 2000

his wife Charlene and their children— Ravi, Rishma and Aarti.

"Got a phone call from Guyana," Lutch said solemnly, without preliminaries, "The old man pass away yesterday."

They all remained silent for a while not knowing what to say, feeling deprived and heartbroken that they were not with Sook at the moment when his soul transmigrated, for better or for worst, to the world beyond.

Sook's grandkids in Belize-1990's
Romain, Ravi, Aarti, Rishma, Liz

ACKNOWLEDGEMENTS

I sincerely thank the following persons for providing photos and/or giving permission for the use of photos they posted online:

1. Johnny R.P. Singh—many photos: loading cane punt; gas lamps; huts; Rudge bicycle; Broadway cigarettes; ploughing rice field, planting rice; cutting rice; Kennedy and Jagan.
2. Fazil Hussain – photo of Anna Regina High Bridge and Anna Regina Rice Factory
3. Hemwant Persaud—photo of women with head kerchiefs/rumaals; grip; battery; poe

Other photos were taken from anonymous sources, to whom I am also grateful, or generated by the author.

ABOUT THE AUTHOR

Karan Chand (aka Chines/ Ghasi) grew up in Anna  Regina, Essequibo Coast, Guyana). By vocation, he has been a teacher all of his adult life. Between 1980 and 1989 he taught at Abram Zuil Secondary School, Alleyne High School, Anna Regina Community High School and Anna Regina Multilateral School.

He has also taught in Belize (formerly British Honduras) in Central America at various secondary and tertiary level educational institutions including the Belize Teachers' Training College and the University of Belize, culminating his career there as a principal at St. Michael's College. In between, he taught in the Turks and Caicos and in the USA.

By avocation, he is a writer and poet and has also written a book of short stories titled, "JIM JONES' JUSTICE and other short stories", and one of poems " I HAD A DREAM an anthology of poems ".

In 2009 Chand migrated to Canada where he has been teaching adult students from all over the world at the Adult Education Centers of the Peel and York District School Boards, Ontario.

Karan is married to Sita and they have two children — Elizabeth and Romain.

He can be contacted at kchand16@hotmail.com